THE
SHAAR
PRESS

THE JUDAICA IMPRINT
FOR THOUGHTFUL PEOPLE

A Jewish perspective –
from the case files
of an eminent
psychiatrist

A
SHAAR
PRESS
PUBLICATION

I

am

BY
RABBI ABRAHAM J. TWERSKI, M.D.

Published by **SHAAR PRESS**
Distributed by MESORAH PUBLICATIONS, LTD.
4401·Second Avenue / Brooklyn, New York 11232 / (718) 921-9000

Distributed in Israel by SIFRIATI / A. GITLER BOOKS
10 Hashomer Street / Bnei Brak 51361

Distributed in Europe by J. LEHMANN HEBREW BOOKSELLERS
20 Cambridge Terrace / Gateshead, Tyne and Wear / England NE8 1RP

Distributed in Australia and New Zealand by GOLDS BOOK & GIFT SHOP
36 William Street / Balaclava 3183, Vic., Australia

Distributed in South Africa by KOLLEL BOOKSHOP
Shop 8A Norwood Hypermarket / Norwood 2196 / Johannesburg, South Africa

ISBN: 0-89906-420-5 Hard Cover
ISBN: 0-89906-421-3 Paperback

Printed in the United States of America by Noble Book Press
Custom bound by Sefercraft, Inc. / 4401 Second Avenue / Brooklyn, N.Y. 11232

I am I

"If I am I because I am I,

and you are you because you are you,

then I am and you are.

But if I am I because you are you,

and you are you because I am I,

then I am not and you are not.**"**

(R' Menachem Mendel of Kotzk)

Author's Introduction

broad spectrum of questions have been addressed to me over a number of years. Some of these questions should appropriately have been posed to a rabbi, whose study of Torah lore would provide the resources for a reply. Many questioners, however, must have felt that their inquiries involved emotional and ideational concepts that are in the realm of psychology rather than theology, but because they also touch upon issues of faith and religious values, may not be adequately answered by someone who draws only upon psychology. Perhaps this is why these issues found their way to me, in the expectation that I would be able to draw upon both my Torah education and psychiatric training to provide satisfactory answers.

Over the years, the same or similar questions came from a number of different people, leading me to conclude that these particular queries may not be unique to certain individuals, but are found in the thoughts of many people. Further research among various groups confirmed this, and ultimately resulted in the idea of making these topics, and my attempts to answer them, more widely available to others who may have harbored them.

This, then, is essentially a book of responsa. The halachic literature abounds with questions that were posed to halachic authorities and the answers which became precedents and the basis for decisions on subsequent problems. This model may serve to address issues of *hashkafah* (Torah perspective) and related psychological problems as well.

However, whereas halachic responsa books invariably begin with the questions and answers, I felt it necessary to provide a somewhat lengthy preface to the responsa, in order to avoid the necessity of repeating certain concepts again and again.

In my first book, *Like Yourself and Others Will Too* (Prentice-Hall, 1978), I postulated that with the exception of those emotional disorders that are a consequence of biochemical changes within the body, the overwhelming number of psychological and/or emotional problems which afflict people can be traced to a single underlying cause: **lack of self esteem.** This term refers to a distorted self-perception whereby a person in fact sees himself as less than he is.

It stands to reason that a satisfactory adjustment to life can be made only if one has a correct perception of reality. Every person is a major part of his own reality, and a delusion about oneself is certain to result in maladjustment. A person who is delusional or hallucinating and reacts to things that do not exist in actuality will run into serious trouble. A person of meager means who purchases costly items because of a delusion that he is a billionaire is obviously going to precipitate much distress for himself. It is no less a distortion of reality if a person who is variously talented and gifted does not recognize his personality assets and bases his behavior and actions on a distorted self-perception, which is essentially a delusion. While delusions of grandiosity are quite rare, delusions of inadequacy are very common, and many inappropriate and psychologically unhealthy behaviors are the result of this misinterpretation of reality. A number of maladaptive behaviors incident to unwarranted low self esteem are described in that book.

In my book, *Let Us Make Man* (CIS, 1987), I further elaborated on this theme and pointed out that low self esteem, which is an undesirable state, should not be confused with humility (*anivus*), which is a highly desirable trait. Indeed, vanity (*gahvah*) is invariably a desperate psychological defense whereby a person attempts to escape from feelings of low self-worth by assuming himself to be superior to everyone else. Positive self-esteem is merely an awareness of one's potential and capabilities, and denial of the truth about oneself cannot be considered virtuous. The Torah, which places the highest value on truth, could not possibly consider deviance from truth to be a virtue. The great sage Hillel, whose humility is considered by the Talmud as second only to that of Moses, said, "If I am here, all is here" (*Sukkah* 53a). Without a proper, healthy sense of "I," there can be no humility.

I also pointed out ways in which a true Torah approach to living is conducive to positive self-esteem, and in response to a number of questions, I will refer to some of these concepts. The pivotal role of a healthy self-esteem requires a bit of analysis of the basic concept of *identity*.

In order to avoid a breach of confidentiality, possible identifying features in the inquiries I received have been altered, but the essential features relevant to the problem have been maintained. If you think you can identify the questioner because his/her problem is like that of someone you know, please bear in mind that there are hundreds of people with similar problems.

Chapter 1

If I am I because I am I,
and you are you because you are you,
then I am and you are.
But if I am I because you are you,
and you are you because I am I,
then I am not and you are not.

n these few cryptic lines Rabbi Mendel of Kotzk condensed the issue of identity to its very essence. A genuine identity cannot be contingent on any external source. I have a bona fide identity only if it is a product of my own self-evaluation. If I am dependent on you or anyone else or anything else for my identity, then I do not have a true identity.

While this may sound simple enough, it is anything but simple. Just what is a self-evaluation that is independent of every external source? I may think of myself as a man or woman, one of which I undoubtedly am, but if I think of myself as a husband or wife, as a father or mother, as a son or daughter, brother or sister, professional, laborer, or businessman, Republican or Democrat, believer or non-believer, citizen of this country or that, are not these part of my identity, albeit they do not all emanate from within? How much can I really say about myself that does not involve a relationship to an external person or object? Is my identity merely an abstraction, much like Plato's ideals, which has no actual existence in the real world? Was Adam the only being to have a true identity, and did he lose it when Eve came on the scene?

Let me think out loud a bit. What do I mean by identity? Does it refer to distinct features whereby something can be identified, like distinguishing someone in a line-up, or recognizing someone among a throng of people? If so, then Adam had no identity, because there was no one with whom he could possibly be confused. And since Eve was significantly different, neither she nor Adam had identities. It was only when additional humans appeared on the scene, some of which were similar to Adam and others to Eve, that the whole concept of identity came into being. Is that what is meant by identity?

Or perhaps Adam did have an identity even as the sole human being on earth, because identity means knowing what you are and who you are, and has nothing to do with distinguishing oneself from others.

Or perhaps we may look at it this way. We can think of identity as meaning that which *I am*, a positive statement, or of being that which *I am not,* which is essentially a negative statement and refers to distinguishing me from others by certain features that indicate that I am not someone or something else.

Do I have an identity, which like my name, or fingerprint, or blood type, accompanies me throughout my life, or does my identity change as my life circumstances change?

It is obvious that it is going to be difficult if not impossible to search for one's identity if we are not even aware how to define identity, or what we are looking for.

Chapter 2

he philosopher Descartes tried to establish what it was that a person can know with absolute certainty. Although one may see many things in one's environment — trees, houses, automobiles, people — and one can be *virtually* certain that they are all real, one cannot be *absolutely* certain of this. We

know that there is a phenomenon of hallucination, wherein a person sees things that do not exist, yet for that person they are very, very real. While it may be absurd to think that one is hallucinating everything one sees, if one wants to be absolutely and scientifically certain of something, he must consider even the most absurd possibility.

Thus, says Descartes, one cannot be certain of anything that one knows by a sense perception, since these are all subject to hallucination. But one does know this much for certain, that even if one is hallucinating, one does exist. A person cannot hallucinate unless he exists to do the hallucinating. Therefore, Descartes concludes, the only thing that one can know for certain is that one exists. This leads to the famous Cartesian doctrine — *cogito ergo sum*, I think, therefore I am.

We might try a somewhat similar approach in trying to establish an identity, a method that will allow us to have an identity that is not contingent on outside sources. It is not because we can argue like Descartes that the outside world does not exist. We can accept the obvious, that people are real and that the things we see are real, yet we should not allow these external realities to be the basis whereby we establish our identity.

Allowing others to establish our identity runs the risk of making one into a chameleon, as one continually changes identities according to what others say one is. At best one becomes a composite of the various identities one assumes. It should be evident that many important decisions in life depend on one's identity, and the decisions made in the presence of a vacillating or poorly defined identity may be less than optimum.

Should not choices in life be an outgrowth of one's identity? Yet, if one has an identity, say, as a physician, then one was not a physician prior to entering medical school. What, then, was the identity of the person who elected to become a physician? Should not marriage and family be based on one's identity? Is it not absurd to choose a marriage partner as a companion for life, when one does not know who one is? Is it not possible that the failure of so many marriages may be attributed to either one or both partners having made a decision wherein they selected someone for themselves or offered themselves to someone without an awareness of their own identity?

The prevalence of externally determined identities appears to be significant. It is only logical to assume that external identities are adopted where there is a vacuum; i.e., where no internal identity exists.

The problem arises that once an externally imposed identity is adopted, that vacuum is filled, which means that there is now no place for an internal identity to develop, even if a person should wish to obtain one. The latter cannot be achieved until the space it is to occupy is first vacated. In other words, we must first divest ourselves of an externally imposed identity in order to develop an internal identity, and this is not a simple feat. There may be an interim during which one is without an identity, and this may prove very threatening to an individual.

For example, lobsters are limited in their growth by a rigid, external shell. In order for a lobster to grow, it must first shed its shell and grow a new shell to accommodate its increased mass. During the interval that the lobster is without its protective shell, it is vulnerable to being devoured by predatory fish. Similarly, shedding one's external identity in order to make room for an internal one can be perceived as being equally menacing.

An individual who has suffered amnesia may suddenly awake to find himself in a strange city. Not knowing who he is or how he arrived there, and also not acquainted with a single soul in the city, he will promptly adopt a name. It appears that a person must have some way of introducing himself to others. Just as one cannot function without a name, so one cannot function without an identity. Hence, the shedding of an external identity in order to adopt an internal one may provoke a great deal of anxiety, so much so, that one may elect to stay with the external identity even if it is not valid.

We may now address two questions: (1) what is an internal identity, and (2) why is its development so uncommon, as the prevalence of external identities appears to indicate?

Chapter 3

ne way to think of an internal identity is that it consists of that which is essential to the definition of oneself if one were isolated on an island, completely out of contact with other people. One could then be defined as a *rational* being, in contrast to all other living things. Whereas animals have some level

of mental activity, we generally assume that they cannot think rationally or understand things, both conceptually and abstractly, the way humans do. Defining oneself as a rational being is not yet an identity, since one shares this with all other humans. However, it is the first step towards an identity.

The essential features of man as a thinking being cannot be overestimated, because it implies that to the extent that one relinquishes rational thought, one demotes oneself from the highest level of humanity. It is said of Napoleon that he despised sleep "because when I am asleep I am not Emperor." If one's very essence is rational thought, then the abdication of rational thought is forfeiting one's very essence. We shall soon see that this plays a crucial role in development of self-esteem.

Rational thought, however, has its limitations, because it cannot proceed beyond the data provided by experience, or by concepts that can be reasonably developed based on such data. Experience brings us into contact with things that have a beginning, hence it is beyond our rational capacity to conceptualize something which has no beginning. An Infinite Being can therefore not be grasped by rational thinking, and requires a leap of faith. The *Midrash* states that the first one to accomplish this leap of faith was the patriarch Abraham, whose rational thinking led him to the conclusion that there must be a first, infinite Supreme Being that is beyond human comprehension, and at this point G-d revealed Himself to him and said, "I am that Being that you seek." Rational thought thus leads one to the awareness that there is a Prime Mover, a Creator, Whom we cannot comprehend rationally. From the Torah aspect, we proceed then from the knowledge of G-d Who revealed Himself to the patriarchs and prophets, and to all of Israel at Sinai.

When one's thinking leads to contemplation of an Infinite Being, which does not fit into the scheme of things as we generally know them, one may totally dismiss it, essentially saying, "I refuse to consider anything that I cannot understand." Alternatively one may say that there can be an existence of something that is beyond one's intellectual grasp. While the leap of faith may be a quantum leap, the *existence* of G-d is not incompatible with rational thought. It is the *nature* of the Supreme Being that is beyond human comprehension, and what one knows about G-d is only what has been revealed to us.

The function or purpose of an item may be a key to its identity; e.g., the function of a car for travel, of a pen for writing, and of a telephone for communicating, help define what these items are. Perhaps understanding the function of a person will help us clarify human identity.

For the Jew, the Revelation at Sinai, as expounded upon in the Scriptures, Talmud and Kabbalah, provides the basis for an internal identity. We are taught that every person has a *neshamah*, a soul of Divine origin, and every person has a special place in Creation. Every individual was created for a specific mission, which is accomplished by fulfillment of Torah and *mitzvos*. From the Torah perspective, it is Torah that gives a person an internal identity: "I am a person created for the specific purpose of fulfilling the Divine will as revealed in the Torah. That is my identity, and that is who I am, whether I am woman or man, rich or poor, healthy or ill, and that is my identity regardless of where I am or whatever I do."

Let us now see how this identity affects one's self image and self-esteem.

Chapter 4

elf-esteem is comprised primarily of two components: *competence* and *worthiness*. The two may, but need not necessarily overlap.

Competence means that one is capable of performing certain actions. Obviously, competence as a component of self-esteem must be defined as relative to that which one is expected to perform. The fact that one cannot paint like Rembrandt or play the violin like Heifetz is generally not considered a deficiency, since one is not expected to perform artistically. Competence in terms of what one is reasonably expected to perform is thus contingent upon one's concept of function, goal, and purpose in life.

Unfortunately, a bit of circular reasoning may occur here. Rather than considering competence in terms of goals and purpose, some people consider goals and purpose in terms of competence; i.e., given what one thinks are one's abilities and capacities, one determines one's goals and purpose. If one does not consider oneself to be musical, one does not contemplate music as a career. If one does not consider oneself capable of understanding Torah, one may eliminate study of Torah as a goal. When certain goals are eliminated, one no longer strives for competence in those areas, hence a vicious cycle develops.

Earlier we have noted that rational thought and the ability to understand are the fundamental identifying characteristics of a human being, and it is therefore impossible to have an identity without these traits. This is probably the foremost reason for the prevalence of self-esteem problems.

We may not appreciate how a small child feels in a world that is dominated by adults. A group of psychologists once conducted an experiment where they built a house that was as proportional to adults as an average house is for little children. The ceilings were forty feet high, the tables and chairs were three times the normal height, the doorknobs almost out of reach, etc. They then introduced several emotionally stable adults into the house, and within several days they began showing neurotic symptoms. Imagine what it must be like to have to struggle to climb in order to sit on a chair or to have to stretch to the utmost in order to reach a doorknob.

It is reasonable to assume that a small child feels completely overwhelmed in this world built for giants. The anxiety of existing in this humongous world would be intolerable, except for the trusted intermediates who provide a bridge between the Lilliputian child and the formidable environment. These trusted intermediates are primarily the parents and the few other adults whom the child has learned to trust.

The anxiety of being in an oversized world without a reliable anchor is akin to being adrift in the sea, clinging to a piece of driftwood. The feeling of helplessness and being at the mercy of life-threatening forces is virtually intolerable, and if one is thrown a lifeline, one would clutch it with one's last bit of energy. That is how a small child perceives his parents and other significant adults. For a child to have a feeling of security, he must see these protective adults as stable, fair, wise, and predictable. Perception of these people as anything less than this would jeopardize his security, and this is something which the child cannot risk.

It is obvious that emotions develop long before rational thought. Hence a child may have many desires which cannot or should not be gratified. Furthermore, there are many occurrences in the world which are not rational, and are not understandable even by the mature mind, let alone a child's mind. It is also a necessity of life that children be taught proper and acceptable behavior, which requires discipline and sometimes punishment. These factors may result in a child developing poor self-esteem.

Suppose a child is confronted with something he cannot understand. Perhaps he desires to eat something which his parents feel is unhealthy or to play with something which is dangerous. If being denied his desired object can be explained to him in a way which he can understand, or even if he can be told and made to understand that "when you grow up you will understand," and is capable of grasping this, his feeling of competence and understanding is not undermined. If either of these do not occur, the child may conclude, "I cannot understand because I am *incapable* of understanding." Repeated occurrences such as this can lead to the child doubting his fundamental capacity to understand, and the child may resign himself to this status of inability to understand, which may then impact on many aspects of his behavior. When one's sense of competence pertaining to rational thought is lacking, the very fiber from which self-esteem is woven and the very foundation of an internal identity are absent.

Nor do children always understand discipline. It is possible for a child to learn that certain acts are wrong, such as running into the street or trying to poke out the eyes of a younger sibling. Punishment for such acts may lead the child to conclude, "These acts are bad," and since they indeed are bad, no harm is done. However, a child may sometimes be punished for something he did not do, or for something which he does not think he did, or he may be punished too severely for a minor infraction. In such cases, the child is not likely to conclude, "My parents are unjust," since this would threaten his security and flood him with anxiety. To preserve his image of his parents as being wise and just, he may conclude that he was somehow deserving of a punishment. If he cannot justify this by an awareness of the commission of a bad act, and therefore cannot think, "My *actions* are bad," his only remaining conclusion is, "*I* am bad." Repetition of such occurrences reinforces one's self-image as being bad, apart from one's actions.

It is possible that parents may favor one child over another for any one of a number of reasons. It is also possible that one child may require greater parental attention, whether it is because the child is younger, sick, or in some way in need of extra care. A sibling who is not at the level of maturity where he can understand this may conclude that his parents love him less, and this, too, contributes to poor self-esteem.

It appears, then, that the roots of poor self-esteem lie in the very nature of a person's coming into the world and living in an environment where things may happen that are beyond the grasp of an immature mind, or that can give him a feeling of being bad or less desirable. In contrast to those schools of psychology who *blame* the parents for the child's failure to develop a positive identity, this can be seen as a hazard of being born into a world of adults. It may be assumed that poor self-esteem can be a natural and frequent occurrence in childhood.

 second major component of self-esteem is a feeling of worthiness.

One of man's unique characteristics and hence a defining feature of his essence is *the ability to make moral free choices*. Animals do not make such choices. Animals are basically impulse driven, and are under the dictates of their bodies' desires. While animals may be trained in certain behaviors, these behaviors are adopted as a result of reward and punishment, and do not reflect moral free choice.

Responding to reward and punishment is not a uniquely human trait. Animals seek pleasure and avoid pain, and when certain acts are associated with pleasure and others with pain, animals can be taught to adopt the former and avoid the latter.

Although an animal is impulse driven; e.g., when hungry it must look for food and it cannot decide, "I am going to fast today." It is possible for an animal to forego gratification of hunger if not foregoing would be painful. For example, a hungry jackal who is foraging for food spies a carcass, but it is in the possession of a ferocious tiger. The jackal will not approach the desired food, not out of conviction that it is wrong to take what belongs to another, but because of fear of being killed by the tiger. Animal trainers teach their animals to associate certain acts with punishment and others with reward, and in this manner desired behavior patterns are established in the animal. This is not moral free choice.

A person who is employed in a large financial concern may devise a method of electronically transferring money from other accounts to his own, thereby amassing great wealth. He realizes, however, that the audit team will probably include an expert on computer crime, who may be able to trace the illegal transfers of funds and detect the theft. This would result in the stolen money being taken from him, plus a penalty of many thousands of dollars, and probably a long prison sentence. Since the risk is formidable, he does not execute his designs. This is not a moral free choice, since it is not a result of consideration of right and wrong, but is determined only by the wish to avoid punishment, which is a trait shared with animals.

The moral concept of right and wrong is a uniquely human characteristic, and every person has a need to do right and avoid wrong. However, the *standards* of right and wrong are subject to great variability. A child who is taught to steal when young may develop a standard wherein theft is right. Values are learned rather than innate. The composition of the human spirit as being composed of a *yetzer tov,* an inclination towards good, and a *yetzer hara,* an inclination towards bad, means that the potential for diametric opposite values exists in the human being, and the ultimate adoption of values is a matter of learning and training.

Worthiness is a consequence of the feeling of having lived up to one's standards, whatever they may be. A child trained to steal will feel worthy and deserving if he becomes a competent thief. He is taught that it is morally right to steal, and that becomes his value.

For the Jew, the value system should be that prescribed by the Torah. These values are not arbitrary, nor did they evolve, nor were they adopted by the consensus of a legislature. They are Divinely ordained, absolute, and are not subject to modification. Good and evil are not determined by the democratic process. Murder, adultery, and theft are evil and will remain evil regardless of what people may wish them to be. The Biblical saga of the city of Sodom, whose moral values were perverse, underscores this point.

Torah values may differ sharply from prevailing secular values, and they are clearly stated in *Ethics of the Fathers.* For example, power does not consist in domination over others, but in self-mastery. Wealth is not how much one owns, but the ability to be content with whatever one has. Honor does not consist of receiving tribute, but of giving respect to others.

It is important to note that while values may be relative and various cultures may adopt certain values and exchange them for others when they wish, the Jew does not have such leeway. The *neshamah* (soul) is an integral part of the person, and its needs are synonymous with its values. Just as an individual cannot have optimum health if he is deprived of any of the body's essential nutrients — vitamin B or C, for example — neither can the *neshamah* be completely satisfied unless its needs — Torah values — are satisfied. Unmet needs of the *neshamah,* just as unmet needs of the body, will result in a "deficiency syndrome" characterized by vague feelings of discontent. If the discontented person is unable to identify the reason for his unhappiness, he may turn to acquiring more money or fame, or to food, alcohol, or other chemicals, in order to relieve his dysphoric state.

The analogy between body nutrients and *neshamah* nutrients is inaccurate in one respect. The body's needs for nutrients can be determined, and providing the body with excess nutrients may be of little or no value, as with huge doses of water-soluble vitamins. Certain vitamins taken in excess may be harmful, as with huge doses of vitamins A or D, or with excessive caloric intake. However, for the *neshamah*, which is of Divine origin, there is no upper limit for its spiritual needs. This is why spiritual growth never comes to an end.

This infinite nature of the *neshamah*'s needs thus creates a situation where one can never say, "I am worthy and deserving because I have achieved my goal of spirituality." There is no finite goal in spirituality. One can never feel that one has done enough, and this is the basis of *anivus* (humility).

Yet, self-esteem is essential to a healthy mental state. The question arises, if a feeling of worthiness is a result of having lived up to one's standards, and if spiritual standards are consequently retreating as one advances, so that one always feels unfulfilled, how can one ever attain a feeling of self-esteem?

We may understand this with an analogy. If a person were selected by the president or other head of state to carry out an important diplomatic mission, one would feel honored by this appointment and by the fact that this head of state has the confidence that one is capable of fulfilling an important mission. One must be aware that one has the capacity to perform as desired, or else be obliged to refuse the honor. One would thus have a good feeling about oneself even before performance of the mission had begun. Devotion to one's country and loyalty would make one carefully evaluate, "Am I fulfilling this mission properly? Could I be doing a better job of it than I am doing? Am I making any mistakes in executing this assignment?" Constant striving to improve one's performance need not depress one's self-esteem and even discovery of a mistake one had made could serve as a stimulus to avoid repetition of such mistakes, and hence result in enhanced performance.

Our great Torah scholars obviously had positive self-esteem. Clearly they had a sense of competence, knowing that they possessed G-d-given talents for an understanding of Torah, and that by virtue of these, they had amassed a comprehensive knowledge. Without such self-esteem, they would hardly have accepted positions of leadership and have rendered authoritative *halachic* decisions which became the basis for Jewish law. Yet they were all models of *anivus*, because with their perception of the infinite growth that lay before them, they realized that they had achieved relatively little.

This may well be the true distinction between healthy self-esteem on the one hand and *gahvah* (vanity) on the other. The latter is considered by the Talmud and by all Jewish ethical writings as an abomination. *Self-esteem is an awareness of "what I can do," whereas vanity is "see what I have done."* Vanity may lead to laziness, to rest on one's laurels, whereas the awareness of one's abilities, coupled with humility, make one realize how much one must yet do, and stimulate a person to greater achievement.

Why does one person say, "Look what I must yet do," and another person say, "Look what I have done?" Perhaps it is because a person who lacks self-esteem and who is unaware of one's capabilities, feels threatened and overwhelmed by the enormity of the challenge of "what I must do." This person may therefore try to achieve a sense of worthiness by focussing on "see what I have already done." In other words, *vanity is a defense against low self-esteem.* Although a vain person is usually regarded as someone who is grandiose and who considers himself superior to others, this is but a superficial facade, whose purpose is to deceive oneself even more than to impress others. This conceit betrays an underlying feeling of incompetency and unworthiness, feelings which are unwarranted and would not be present if the person had a correct self-perception.

Other aspects of self-esteem will be discussed in responses to individual problems.

Chapter 6

et us return now to the formulation of the Rabbi of Kotzk, "If I am I." If I define my identity, which consists of my concept of man as a rational being, of a valid awareness of my capabilities, and, as a Jew, of the Torah standards which are to serve as my goals in life, then I can have *my own identity*. I must,

of course, have adequate input as to what constitutes Torah standards, and this is where Torah study and guidance by Torah authorities is essential. I may need some help in discovering my potential. But availing myself of these sources of help does not mean that others are determining my identity. Only I can do that, if I so choose.

Lack of awareness of my capabilities or establishing unrealistic standards may result in feelings of incompetence or unworthiness which may preclude my developing an identity of my own. In such cases, I may rely on others to determine my identity. I may see myself as being worthy only when others tell me I am worthy, and this may lead to "people-pleasing." I may be tossed about like a ship in a stormy sea, being at the mercy of everyone else's appraisal. I may be one thing for my spouse, another thing for my parents, yet another for my children, my siblings, my friends, my teachers, my employer, my employees, etc. I am nothing unless others tell me what I am, and this is what the Rabbi of Kotzk meant that "If I am I only because you are you," and you tell me what I am, then "I am *not,*" meaning I do not have a true identity.

Being rational, however, is not as simple as it may appear. A narrow definition of man as an intellectual person; i.e., of having knowledge and being able to process data, and even to be able to form concepts and think in the abstract does not satisfy the criterion of "a rational being," because the latter means that one *acts* according to purely rational decisions.

A child's decision to eat something sweet is obviously an impulse-driven rather than a rational decision. The adult who should be avoiding sweets and goes against one's better judgment is similarly making an impulse-driven decision. However, there are many decisions that people make which are not overtly impulse-driven and which may appear rational, but are nevertheless determined emotionally. Our desires have an incredibly powerful impact on our thinking, and we may be easily deluded into thinking that a given decision was rational. As Rabbi Dessler points out (*Michtav Me'Eliyahu I*), when a person consults the *Shulchan Aruch* to see whether it is permissible to play chess on Shabbos, his preference is clear, and unless the *halachah* is explicitly stated, he is left to draw conclusions by inference from other *halachos*. His reasoning faculties will tend to lead to the conclusion that he desires. While this is certainly utilizing one's reasoning powers, the decision may not be a purely *rational* one.

Purely rational decisions may be difficult to come by, since everyone has many desires that can affect and distort one's reasoning to a greater or lesser degree. A diligent search for the truth, trying to set aside one's personal preferences, is certainly of help, but pure, absolute objectivity may not be within human grasp. It may be necessary to consult someone who is not subject to one's desires and biases to get a more objective perspective.

Just as the emotion of desire for something can be a distorting factor, so can the emotion of fear. People may be deterred from purely rational conclusions by fear of the unknown, fear of failure, and even fear of success.

Obviously, the degree of self-confidence one has is a major determinant in whether one is subject to fear. A self-confident person will undertake things with an anticipation of success, and a person with a healthy self-esteem will not be deterred by the possibility of an unsuccessful result. While failure is unpleasant, it need not be perceived as so overwhelmingly disastrous that one must avoid it at all costs. A person with self-esteem will therefore take reasonable risks, knowing the outcome is not always under one's control, and that failure is not a reflection on one's worth.

Fear may be as much a cause of lack of self-confidence as it is a consequence. A person who lacks self-esteem because of a feeling of unworthiness may be hesitant to risk failure. In order to justify his inaction he may conclude, "I lack the abilities to achieve."

One young woman who was admitted for treatment for alcoholism was obsessed with the idea that she had suffered brain damage. All assurances that she had not sustained any brain impairment failed to relieve her of her conviction. Further analysis revealed that she actually *wished* to be diagnosed as having brain damage, because she would then be relieved of the burdens associated with recovery. As a brain-damaged person, she could not be expected to overcome the urge to drink, nor be expected to complete her education or hold a responsible job.

Fear of success can be as significant a deterrent to constructive action as fear of failure, since success is likely to create new responsibilities and obligations.

The conclusion "I am unable to do this" may appear to be a rational decision, but if it is motivated by fear, it may be less than truly rational, just as the decision to do something which will satisfy a desire may not be a fully rational decision.

The necessary components for a true identity; i.e., being a truly rational being, with a valid self-awareness, and having appropriate standards and values, are thus not to be assumed as being universally present. To the contrary, this attainment may require a great deal of diligent effort.

It is related that the chassidic master, the Seer of Lublin, sent some of his disciples to Tomashov, to find Rabbi Mendel and bring him to Lublin. The disciples were unable to find any Mendel in Tomashov who appeared to be the person desired by the Seer. One night they concealed themselves in the *beis medrash*, and towards midnight they saw a young man enter the empty room, recite *Tehillim (Psalms)* with great *kavanah* (concentration), then go to the Ark and open it, pleading passionately and tearfully with G-d, "Show me the truth." The disciples emerged from hiding and asked him if his name might be Mendel, and when he answered affirmatively, they told him that the Seer of Lublin had requested that he come to him. This was the future Rebbe of Kotzk, who said that there is nothing else worthwhile in life except the pursuit of truth, and since truth is synonymous with G-dliness, the attempt to become closer to G-d is essentially the pursuit of truth.

It is therefore completely compatible with Rabbi Mendel's character that he formulated the concept, "If I am I." It is no mean achievement to have a true identity. The pursuit of such truth requires much effort, much denial of personal gratification, and tolerance of much frustration.

Chapter 7

he prevalence of problems resulting from low self-esteem makes one wonder whether this is a new phenomenon or were things always this way, and if it is a new phenomenon, why?

As one reviews the works of *mussar* and *chassidus*, one cannot but be impressed by the greater emphasis on self-esteem in the more recent writings. The Torah tells us that the battle against Amalek is continuous from generation to generation (*Exodus* 17:16). If we see Amalek as the personification of evil, this tells us that the struggle against evil changes from generation to generation. It may very well be that the problem of self-esteem was not as severe in previous times.

One of the recent teachers of *mussar*, Rabbi Yitchak Isaac Sher wrote a beautiful essay on the greatness of man. His words could well have been written by a modern psychologist.

> All behavior, whether physical or spiritual, public or private, is conducted and is based on one's self-evaluation. A person with poor self-esteem has no self-respect, and disparages life as a whole. He is even prone to be reckless in caring for his very safety. Not so the one who has self-esteem, who recognizes himself for what he is, who therefore values life and tries to improve and develop himself with all his energy, and to elevate life itself.
>
> . . . Therefore the most important principle in one's life is to recognize and know the value of a person as set forth in the Torah . . . From the awareness of one's greatness, one can have an awareness of the spiritual goals and duties of the human being . . . (The Talmud says), you shall emulate G-d. Just as He is merciful, you should be merciful, etc., which is the fundamental principle underlying all ethics . . . (Without a correct self-evaluation) how could a person possibly compare oneself even remotely to G-d?

There are, of course, references to this theme in earlier writings, but nowhere is it expanded as in the more recent works. Perhaps there was not as great a need for this in earlier times.

Life in the *shtetl* may have been more conducive to self-esteem. Today we note the pursuit of finding one's "roots," whether by ethnic groups or as evidenced by the popularity of geneologic trees. Forty years ago one would have been hard pressed to find a geneologist, whereas today there are many advertisements of services to trace one's family tree. In the *shtetl*, one's roots were well known, because the family had been living there or in a nearby hamlet within walking distance for several generations. As cities grew in size and complexity and took on a metropolitan character, the individual's identity in the community eroded. This has reached its apogee in the modern, mobile industrialized society, where remaining in one community for a lifetime is a rarity. Indeed, a family may move several times, and the impact of this, especially on young children who must repeatedly overcome the feeling of being the "new kid on the block," cannot be overestimated.

Prevailing secular-scientific-cultural ideas can have a great impact on self-esteem. Prior to the sixteenth century, when it was assumed that the earth was the center of the universe and that all the heavenly bodies revolved around it, it was rather easy for one to feel important in being at the focal point of everything. The Copernican revolution deprived man of this vantage point, and as astronomy progressed, we became increasingly aware that we inhabit one of the lesser planets revolving about a third rate star, and that the entire solar system would barely be evident on the celestial map covering unimaginable trillions of miles of space. Our planet is hardly a speck of dust in the known expanse of the universe.

Having been deprived of his focal point in the universe, man could take solace in the fact that for reasons known only to Him, G-d chose to place His special creation on this tiny speck of dust. The secular world was rocked by the theories of evolution, which denied special creation and relegated man to a very lowly origin.

Man had hardly begun to deal with this onslaught to his ego, when the wave of modern psychology, led by Freud, informed people that their concept that they were free agents to determine how they would live and behave was just a figment of their imagination. Man, Freud said, is nothing but a conglomeration of impulses derived from the protoplasm of which one is composed, and these impulses interact and conflict with one another, resulting in the ultimate dominance of the most powerful impulses which then govern and determine one's behavior. The logical extension of this is that a human being is little more than an automaton, hardly responsible for one's behavior.

The Torah-observant Jew has no problem with the findings of astronomy, but categorically rejects both denial of special creation and psychologic determinism. We believe that we are expressly created for a special mission and purpose, and that we have absolute freedom of will in moral behavior. All this notwithstanding, the depression of self-esteem secondary to Darwinian and Freudian theories that has affected humanity as a whole has had a ripple effect and an impact on the self-esteem of even the Torah-true Jew.

Just as basic halachah does not change over time, neither do the principles of ethics. However, just as one must consult the works of the modern *poskim* (halachic authorities) on questions involving technologies that were unknown in earlier times, so one must consult the recent Torah authorities on ethics. Just as contemporary halachah has its origin in the Scriptures and Talmud, which requires proper application to present-day problems, so does ethics have its origin in the ethical principles of the Scriptures or Talmud.

It is questionable whether we would find among the earlier ethicists a statement made by the great modern proponent of *mussar*, Rabbi Shmuel Weintraub of Slobodka:

"If we analyze the words of the Talmud, we can see that they illuminate for us a fundamental principle: the awareness of G-d is contingent upon a self-awareness."

This is not really a novel statement, and can be found in the Scriptures: "From my flesh I can perceive G-d" (*Job* 19:26).

The greatness of man is explicitly stated in the Talmud. "Man is precious because he was created in the Divine image" (*Ethics of the Fathers* 3:14). But this fact in itself is not enough, and would be of little value unless a person recognized his own grandeur. Therefore the Talmud continues, "His preciousness was made known to him, that he was created in the Divine image" (*ibid.*). The principles of self-esteem can thus be found in the earliest Torah writings, but their elaboration was not as essential as in our times, when the human being has been subject to the utmost degradation.

The Torah dictates that a criminal who was executed must be given prompt burial, because the display of a human being who was executed is an affront against G-d, since man was created in the image of G-d (*Deuteronomy* 21:23). By the same token, the decadence of any human being has an impact on all others, since we share so many similarities.

The decadence and moral corruption of modern society has significantly impacted on everyone's self-esteem. It is most difficult for a person to aspire to spiritual heights within a culture that has deteriorated to a sub-animal level, sanctioning perversities and practices that are beneath those of brute beasts. Every bit of reinforcement and encouragement is therefore necessary to lift a person out of his surroundings, and to enable him to be the crown of Creation that he was intended to be.

Correspondences

Correspondence 1

As a *baal teshuvah* studying in Israel, I am a bit confused about what is happening.

In the United States, observant people and non-observant people are able to live side-by-side without any bitterness. My parents do not keep a kosher home, but when I come home, my mother respects my practices and has separate dishes for me. We even joke about it.

In Israel it hurts me to see the bitterness between the religious and non-religious. Some of my yeshivah friends go out to demonstrate against violation of religion, but I just stay behind. Is it wrong of me to do so? Why can't people here respect each other's way of life as they do in the United States?

You have touched upon a very painful issue. It is somewhat reminiscent of the case where the rabbi listened to a litigant in a case and said, "You are absolutely right." The other litigant then presented his position, the polar opposite of the first, and again the rabbi said, "You are absolutely right." The rabbi's wife overheard this and said to him, "Two diametrically opposite positions cannot both be absolutely right," to which the rabbi responded, "You are absolutely right."

There is a major difference between the United States and Israel. In the United States, people who observe Shabbos, for example, do not restrict others from going to the theater on Friday night or using public transportation on Shabbos. In Israel, some non-observant people complain that their rights are being infringed upon by restrictions imposed upon them by a minority. They say that if they do as they please on Shabbos, they are not infringing on anyone else's rights to abstain from doing so. When they argue that this is not the way a democracy should operate, one may say that they are absolutely right.

Torah-observant Jews, however, believe that Israel is our country not because of Zionist nationalism, but because it is the land given to us by G-d. They could never have accepted Herzl's proposed solution to the problem of anti-Semitism in Europe by establishing a Jewish state in Uganda.

With the only claim to Israel based on the Torah, they point to the dire warnings in the Torah that unless its inhabitants observe the Torah, they will be driven from the Land. For someone to say that he has the right to do as he wishes as long as he does not impinge on others is thus analogous to someone in a boat drilling a hole under his own seat and claiming that it will not affect others. Torah-observant people are of the conviction that we lost our sovereignty due to our deviance from the Torah, and that such divergence constitutes a grave threat to all of Israel, whether observant or non-observant.

The efforts to intervene and prevent others from violating the Torah are sometimes characterized by tactics of force, which is extremely distasteful. Yet, no one would criticize a parent for spanking a child who ran out into the street or did something else which is extremely dangerous. It is obviously the parent's obligation to do whatever is necessary to prevent the child from harming himself. Torah-observant Jews who see the violation of Torah as being self-destructive, and feeling that those who violate Torah are unaware of this, believe that they have an obligation similar to that of the parent to the child who is unaware that what he is doing is harmful.

However, I happen to believe that there are more effective tactics than some that have been employed. For example, the Baal Shem Tov once observed someone violating the Shabbos. He promptly concluded that he must have been guilty of a similar violation himself, in accordance with his teaching that any improper act one sees in another person is a reflection of one's own defects. He then did an intensive soul searching to discover how he had in any way been guilty of violating the Shabbos.

It is understandable that people to whom Shabbos is dear and sacred may be extremely irritated when others violate Shabbos at their doorsteps, and they may take this as a provocation. However, while some shout "Shabbos!" only at those who transgress the Shabbos, they may be so distracted by this that they may forget to shout "Shabbos!" at themselves, the way the Baal Shem Tov did.

If there is one factor common to all humanity, it is the right to the pursuit of happiness. While different people may have varying concepts of happiness, everyone seeks it. People who do not feel that they can get happiness in any other way, may in their desperation turn to alcohol, drugs, or any of many hedonistic methods to get it.

I am firmly convinced that if people who were Torah-observant were truly happy and manifested this happiness, everyone would follow suit. If we read the great works on Shabbos, such as the

Siduro shel Shabbos (The Order of Shabbos), we realize that proper observance of Shabbos would provide the ultimate in happiness. With the onset of Shabbos one would feel totally relieved of all worries: *Vayechulu*, everything is in a state of completion. There is absolutely no carryover from the problems of the work week. One is keenly aware of the Divine angels who visit the home, and the chant of *Shalom Aleichem Malachei Hashalom* is sung with the feeling that there is true peace in the home.

Shabbos should be a truly spiritual day, in which the physical self is appeased by the traditional tasty dishes, so that the body's needs do not interfere with the *neshamah*'s (soul) achieving spiritual heights in prayer and in Torah study. One feels oneself to be in the imminent presence of G-d in an intimate relationship of *Lecha Dodi Lekras Kallah* (Come, my beloved to greet the Shabbos bride). If Shabbos is the queen-bride, then the Jew is the king-bridegroom.

If this were the way that Shabbos were observed, the Shabbos-observant Jew would glow with joy, and his face would radiate happiness. Anyone observing a *Shomer-Shabbos* would plead to be helped to share this ecstasy of the paradisical experience, which is indeed referred to as *Mei'ein Olam Haba*, a taste of the bliss of the Eternal World.

Is this, however, the way we observe Shabbos, even the most stringent of us? Do we radiate joy and happiness throughout the day? Is there true peace in every corner of our homes? Do we indeed forget all our work-week worries? Do we experience the absolute of love and brotherliness that should characterize Shabbos, free of all pettiness, greed, envy and *lashon hara* (gossip or slander)? Do we observe Shabbos the way it is described in *Siduro shel Shabbos*? Have we made Shabbos so beautiful, that its attraction should be irresistible, far greater than the attractive force of the most powerful magnet?

We must regretfully admit that while we may appropriately observe the *halachos* of Shabbos, we are far from making it irresistibly attractive. Like the Baal Shem Tov, we might profit by shouting "Shabbos!" at ourselves and realize that we, too, are derelict in its observance. Whereas we do not drive our cars on Shabbos, we are nevertheless grossly deficient in its spiritual observance. Let us make Shabbos into the *Mei'ein Olam Haba* that it is supposed to be, and there will then be little need to shout "Shabbos!" at others. They will flock to us to learn how to participate in its bliss.

What is true of Shabbos is true of all Torah observances. If we have not made Torah observance irresistibly attractive, it is we that are remiss.

The greatest *kiruv* (bringing others to observance of Torah) is achieved by example, and we still have much work to accomplish in that direction.

Correspondence 2

In your book *Let Us Make Man* you distinguish between self-esteem and *gahvah* (vanity). I think I understood your point, but I still have some difficulty in thinking well of myself when *mussar* (ethics) requires me to think that I am absolutely nothing. Could you elaborate on this?

I don't know that I can add much to what I wrote in *Let Us Make Man*, but I will nevertheless try to elaborate a bit.

What *mussar* advocates is *sheviras halev*, the concept of being broken-hearted because one has not done enough. Imagine a person who was assigned a task of transferring a huge pile of bricks, and the employer came to check on him after two weeks, only to find that he had not transferred more than two out of the several thousand bricks. What would the employer say to him, and how would this person feel about himself and the paucity of his work? On the other hand, if the person had been disabled by accident or illness, he would not feel badly about himself for having done so little, nor would the employer fault him for dereliction, because he was physically unable to do the work.

We cannot have the requisite *sheviras halev* and awareness of how little we have done unless we are aware of how much we can do. If I am tone deaf I cannot be expected to perform musically, and if I am color blind I cannot be expected to be a painter.

Self-esteem means an awareness of one's competence and capabilities. Only with the proper self-esteem can there be *anivus* (humility). Someone who lacks self-esteem will not feel that he has not done enough. To the contrary, he will resign himself to having done whatever is within his capacity and is likely to be self satisfied.

We do not begin to appreciate our enormous capabilities. For example, the *seforim* (Torah literature) state that "the mind can control the heart." Most people would say that the reverse is true, and that the heart rules the mind.

In the 1960s a method of biofeedback treatment was introduced into medicine. Prior to this it was assumed that many bodily functions are not subject to voluntary control, so that, for example, a person cannot dilate or constrict his pupils the way he can raise or lower his hand, or cannot control the heart rate voluntarily. With biofeedback, which is nothing more than a self-training method utilizing some electronic monitoring, a person can achieve voluntary control over virtually every bodily function. If it were helpful from a medical perspective, a person could learn how to simultaneously constrict the left pupil while dilating the right. By using a biofeedback monitored electroencephalogram, a person can learn to control his brain waves voluntarily.

This is just one example of the enormous capacities inherent in the human system, and these can be harnessed for constructive purposes.

I suspect that many of our *gedolim* (Torah giants) had learned the art of self-regulation without the aid of the biofeedback electronic gadgetry. For example, the *Tzaddik* of Sanz was able to function with very little sleep, and when asked how he did so, he responded, "A fast runner can traverse a distance in a fraction of the time it takes someone else. I am a fast sleeper, and I can get six hours sleep in one hour."

Studies in human sleep have revealed that there are several stages of sleep, characterized by different brain wave patterns on the electroencephalograph. Normally it may take forty-five minutes to build up to the stage of sleep known as REM (rapid eye movement) which is in itself very brief. If it were possible for a person to immediately achieve an hour of REM sleep, it might well be possible to function with only one hour's sleep.

I believe that our *gedolim* trained themselves to eat, sleep, think, concentrate, and perhaps even feel, bringing all of these under greater voluntary control. It was this extraordinary self-discipline that gave them the self-mastery that enabled them to become *ge'onim* (geniuses) and *tzaddikim*.

One cannot undertake such a self-discipline unless one knows one has the capacity to do so. Self-esteem means that one has a correct understanding of the raw material with which one was endowed.

The *neshamah* is an integral of the Supreme Being, and is limited only by the restrictions of the physical body which it inhabits. How little we appreciate of the enormous heights which we can attain! The reason we do not do so is either because we are unaware of our capacities, are simply too lazy to make the effort, or both.

For all his greatness, the *Tzaddik* of Sanz is known to have said, "I was given a fine *neshamah*. Too bad I did not exploit it properly." The awareness of what a *neshamah* is results in self-esteem. The awareness of how relatively little one has accomplished, compared to its virtually infinite capacities, even though one has objectively achieved a great deal, constitutes the *sheviras halev* and the *anivus* that *mussar* teaches us.

Lack of self-esteem is the cause of *gahvah*. How could one boast of one's achievements and think of oneself as deserving of praise if one knows that one had accomplished a mere fraction of one's potential? Rather than be proud, one would be deeply embarrassed by how little has been done. It is only when one thinks oneself to have fully discharged one's obligations and to have performed beyond the call of duty that one is subject to *gahvah*.

We can therefore understand why *gahvah* is likely to result in inaction and resting on one's laurels, whereas self-esteem will stimulate one to ever greater achievements.

Correspondence 3

... When I was sixteen I went to New York on a music scholarship. I played the violin, and through a series of events I became a *baal teshuvah*. By the way, your book, *Let Us Make Man*, was very helpful to me.

Our family is second generation Reform. My father is a successful businessman, and my two older brothers are in the business with him. I never liked business, and was planning to make music my livelihood.

When I became observant, I realized I knew nothing of Torah, and enrolled in a yeshivah. My father was furious, because he had barely made peace with my choosing music over his business, and now I had set my music aside in order to learn Torah. Furthermore, he is violently opposed to my being *frum*. My mother is rather neutral, but she doesn't dare disagree with my father.

I married at twenty-two, and I am now twenty-five, and we have one child. My wife teaches, and I earn a little by giving violin lessons. I spend most of my time at the yeshivah.

I visit my parents once or twice a year, but it is extremely unpleasant. My father screams at me. I have tried to explain to him why it is important to do the will of G-d, but he says I've been brainwashed and refuses to listen.

I have been told that since my father refuses to become *shomer mitzvos* (observant), I am exempt from the *mitzvah* of *kibbud av* (parental respect). I really don't think I have to accept all that abuse from him . . .

I am greatly upset by people who offer halachic opinions when they are completely unqualified to do so. In our prayer for forgiveness, we list our various transgressions, among which is "I have given bad advice." Whereas only a frankly wicked person would purposely mislead someone, many people try to be helpful and give advice. It should be realized that giving bad advice is as forbidden by the Torah as eating *treifah*, and just as an observant person is meticulous about the *kashrus* of what he eats and will refrain from eating anything that he is uncertain about, so one should be meticulous about whether the advice he is giving is indeed valid. Someone who lacks qualification in halachic opinion should maintain silence. Although I have *semichah* (ordination), I generally do not render any halachic decisions that I believe should be made only by a *posek* (halachic authority) who is constantly engaged in halachah.

Whoever told you that you are exempt from *kibbud av* because your father is non-observant is grossly mistaken. You are absolutely obligated to give your father the utmost respect, regardless of how severely he berates you. The Talmud tells, in laudatory terms of a gentile, who was sitting with high Roman officials, when his mother, who was mentally ill, approached him and tore off his clothes, slapped him in the face, and spat at him, but he restrained himself and did not react (*Kiddushin* 31a). That is how far parental respect is carried.

It was never more true that a little knowledge is dangerous. Your informant undoubtedly knows about the halachah that if a person is a *rasha* (wicked) and sinful, he forfeits the right to parental respect. Note that this does not refer to someone who is "sinful" but someone who is a *rasha*, an appellation which, according to the Chazon Ish, does not apply to anyone in our time.

The Chazon Ish states that a person cannot be considered a *rasha* unless he rejects appropriate rebuke. Already in the time of the Talmud, the Sages were uncertain if there was anyone who was competent to deliver rebuke, and certainly in our time, there is no one who can meet this qualification. Therefore, says the Chazon Ish, in the absence of someone competent to deliver rebuke, there is no one who can be termed a *rasha*.

Your father was raised with certain standards which he adopted. Granted, according to Torah, these standards are erroneous, but this is what he was taught and what he has believed all his life. You have brought some new ideas into the home. Is it realistic for you to expect your father to adopt them?

Many commentaries ask why we single out the test of the patriarch Abraham with the sacrifice of Isaac as the greatest example of *mesiras nefesh* (personal sacrifice). Indeed, the patriarch was put through ten tests of his loyalty and devotion to G-d, and this one was considered the most severe of all. There are many incidents in Jewish history that demanded equal or possibly greater *mesiras nefesh* than that of Abraham. One example is the story of Channah and her children — she witnessed the murder of her seven sons as a result of urging them to accept martyrdom rather than to display any obeisance to an idol.

Rabbi Shmuelevitz explains that once Abraham came to the awareness of the true G-d, he constantly preached against idolatry. Of all types of idol worship forbidden by the Torah, one of the greatest abominations is human sacrifice. It stands to reason that Abraham sharply condemned human sacrifice as being absolutely antithetical to Divine worship, something which G-d totally despises. After preaching vehemently against human sacrifice for more than a century, Abraham was now told to bring his son as an offering. If he did so, he would now have to publicly admit that everything that he had advocated and preached for the past hundred years was wrong. Anyone of lesser devotion to G-d than Abraham could not have withstood the test of admitting that he had spent an entire lifetime in error, and that those whom he had criticized and condemned were actually in the right, whereas he was wrong. This was the supreme test of Abraham's loyalty to G-d, and this was his greatness.

You appear to be disappointed that your father is unwilling to accept your way of life, and to admit that he has been living his entire life in error. Is it realistic to expect your father to be as great as the Patriarch? Do any of us even remotely approach him?

I suggest that you learn the laws of *kibbud av* in the *Shulchan Aruch*. You will discover that when you disagree with your father because he is violating halachah, and you wish to point this out to him, you must do this while maintaining an attitude of great respect for him. While you are not permitted to violate halachah even if he asks you to do so, you must nevertheless make every effort to avoid offending him.

Correspondence 4

I am writing to you because I think any other psychiatrist would really think I'm crazy.

My problem is that I do not have any problems. I am happily married and we have two lovely children. I started a business several years ago, and this has prospered far beyond my expectations. My wife and I have many friends, and we are really lacking for nothing.

While we are an observant family, I see people who are much more observant than we, who have multiple problems; financial, health, etc. I cannot believe I am more deserving than they are. I remember learning in yeshivah that some people are given reward in this world for the few *mitzvos* they may have done, and are then excluded from the Eternal World, and it is an unpleasant thought that I may fit into that category.

I live in fear, or maybe dread is a better word, that something is going to happen, that things simply cannot continue being this good for me. I have begun to react to the telephone ringing with anxiety that it is a report that something terrible has happened. I know that I am far from perfect, and that I have done things that were not permissible by Torah, but if I told the average psychiatrist about this, he would laugh at me. I hope you will understand.

 No one knows the Divine system of accounting and why some people who appear to be deserving of reward are subject to much distress. However, questions about Divine justice should only occur when bad things happen to good people, since this appears incompatible with Divine benevolence, and we must then exercise our faith that all is truly just, even though it is beyond our comprehension. When things are compatible with Divine benevolence, this should cause no problem.

It is true that we should not consider ourselves to be *tzaddikim*, deserving of reward. However, G-d's benevolence is such that He may give of His bounty even if people are not fully deserving. Furthermore, just as descendants of wealthy people have a legitimate right to the riches their ancestors earned, we have every right to *zechus Avos*, the merits that our ancestors bequeathed to us.

While we do not ask for reward by virtue of things we have done, because this would constitute *gahvah* (vanity) for thinking we had properly discharged our duties, we may ask for Divine benevolence so that we may have the ability to do *mitzvos*. When a person is in distress, one cannot pray properly, study properly, be of service to others, or fulfill *mitzvos* properly. Your prayers should be for continued success and good fortune so that you may continue to perform the *mitzvos* of the Torah.

The single mission of the *yetzer hara* is to deter people from Torah and *mitzvos,* and how it accomplishes this goal is immaterial. Some people are subjected to intense temptation of one kind or another, while others may be stressed with depressive thoughts that may drain their energies. The anxiety you are experiencing may well be the way the *yetzer hara* may be trying to deter you from doing *mitzvos.* You may set these kinds of thoughts aside, just as you would if the *yetzer hara* tempted you to do anything else that was against the Torah.

When you give your children something that makes them happy, not only do they enjoy it, but you also take pleasure in their enjoyment. Similarly, G-d is pleased when His children enjoy the gifts He gives them, as long as they use them properly according to His will.

If you have been blessed with favorable circumstances, enjoy them and give thanks to G-d for his kindness. The Torah Commandment "You shall eat and be satisfied and shall thank G-d for the good land He has given to you" (*Deuteronomy* 8:10) is to be applied to all other Divine blessings. Continue your study of Torah and performance of *mitzvos,* especially utilizing the means you have been given for *tzedakah* and *gemilas chasadim,* and may G-d continue to bless you with all that is good.

Correspondence 5

My husband is a teacher in the secular department of a yeshiva, and is himself a yeshiva graduate. One of his former students, a very bright young man, became close to my husband during high school, and has become like a member of our family. He is now eighteen and is in the *beis medrash* (full-time Talmudic student). His father is a highly respected *ben-Torah* (scholar).

About a year ago, this young man underwent a sudden behavior change. He began talking loudly and without letup, said things and used words that were out of character for him, and in general acted very foolishly. No one knew what to make of it, and it passed in about a week. He felt very bad about the way he acted, and for a few weeks after that appeared depressed, but then seemed to return to normal.

About a month ago the same thing happened, but with greater intensity. His parents were beside themselves, and I suggested taking him to a doctor but they refused. The father kept him at home and took time to watch over him. They thought that because he is close with us and respects my husband, perhaps we could have some restraining influence on him, and he stayed in our house for two days. It was terrible! I didn't believe this young man even knew such words. We couldn't get him to go to sleep at night, and

I gave him a sleeping pill. This episode finally passed after about ten days.

My husband and I have talked with his family about taking him to a psychiatrist, but the father is adamant in his refusal. He says that this is just a phase and will not recur. He does not believe in psychiatrists and says they only cause trouble, and he does not want this young man to be labelled as "crazy."

We like this young man, and we know he needs professional help. What can we do, and what is our obligation?

 While it is risky to make a diagnosis from a third-hand report, the behavior you describe is so classic that it is possible to safely conclude that this young man has a definite psychiatric problem of a mood disorder. He may have episodes of hyperactivity or depression, or both. Fortunately, there is now a very effective treatment to bring this condition under control. Without treatment, there is great likelihood of recurrence, with possible further intensification of the bizarre behavior.

The responsibility rests with the family, and as a friend you can only suggest, but you cannot actually do anything without the parents' consent. If the young man wishes to seek treatment on his own, he is of age to do so without the parents' consent, and you could then be of assistance to him. In such conditions, however, it is not likely that the patient seeks treatment on his own.

It is most unfortunate that the father is so resistant to treatment. I believe that this resistance is the result of several factors. Firstly, some people may be terribly frightened by the diagnosis of mental illness, and they may just deny its existence, giving all kinds of explanations for what is happening. As soon as the episode passes, they reassure themselves that all is well and that it will never recur. They may think that exposure to psychiatric treatment will make a person feel he is "crazy."

Secondly, there is great concern among families that if word of psychiatric treatment ever leaks out, it would jeopardize the young man's chances of a *shidduch* (marriage). Furthermore, it will not only affect him, but may stigmatize the entire family as having a condition to beware of. I frequently receive calls regarding the advisability of doing a *shidduch* with someone in whose family there has been a case of mental illness.

I must digress here to share some important information. While it is true that certain types of mental illness can be hereditary, awareness of a case in the family need not be grounds for rejecting a *shidduch*. The incidence of the group of related psychiatric disorders — depression, phobias, anxiety disorder, obsessive-compulsive disorder — among Jews is quite high, and it is rare to find a family that does *not* have a case. This problem may have been covered up, or just written off as an eccentricity. The choice is then whether to do a *shidduch* with a family where there is a *known* case of an emotional disorder, or with one where it has been concealed. It can rarely be totally avoided.

While I can understand the family's concern, withholding treatment cannot be justified. As a friend, you should try to impress this upon them. Furthermore, they are overlooking the fact that there may be recurrences of bizarre behavior of such magnitude that the problem will be exposed in a much more unpleasant way than if it were to be known that the young man was under psychiatric care.

Let us assume, however, that there will be no recurrence for the next several years. You should inform the parents that when they will do a *shidduch* with this young man, you will have to ask a *she'eilah* (pose a question) of a *posek* (halachic authority) on whether you are obligated to inform the girl's family of your awareness of the young man's previous episodes. The halachic position may well be that in compliance with the Biblical commandment, "Do not stand idly by your neighbor's blood" (*Leviticus* 19:16), from which the Talmud derives that one is obligated to divert harm from another person, you may be required to notify the other party of important information you think may have been withheld. From the aspect of common decency think of your daughter marrying a man who, after they have three children, has a major psychotic break, and you then discover that some people knew he had experienced serious emotional problems in the past, but they had not cautioned you. How would you feel towards them?

I do not understand what kind of concept people have of marriage if they are willing to base it on frank dishonesty. From the point of view of secular law, withholding of significant information may make the marriage contract null and void on the basis of fraud, and even if this may not be so in halachah, it is certainly a poor way to begin what should be the most trusted and intimate relationship in one's life.

Hopefully, the parents will reconsider and avail themselves of psychiatric treatment for the young man. If they do not, you will have discharged your obligation.

Correspondence 6

... I am twenty-nine, have been married for two years, and we have a six-month old baby.

When I met my husband, I was on the rebound from a broken engagement, and I was in a very depressed state. I was vulnerable and I knew it, and I realized that I should not become seriously involved for a while. However, my parents manipulated me like you cannot believe, and my future husband joined in the manipulation. I cannot disown my responsibility for getting into this marriage because I was a mature adult, but you have no idea of the pressures I was put under. We left for Israel, where my husband is now in a *kollel*. There are major differences between my husband and myself, and our marriage is not a pleasant one. I am consumed with anger at my parents for pressuring me into the marriage, and I am also angry at my husband for his share in this. Under the constant stress of anger, I don't see how this marriage can survive.

Nonetheless, we have the baby to consider, and I am willing to do anything to see if the marriage can be salvaged. I don't think I can do this while we are at each other's throats. I act, he reacts. He acts, I react. I've suggested a separation, during which I will see a therapist and get myself straightened out. My husband has agreed to therapy, recognizing that he has a bunch of his own issues. I think we should separate for a while, see our therapists, get our individual acts together, and then we could see someone together to ascertain if we have a relationship. My husband agrees to everything except the separation. What do you think is best?

 I think the idea of therapy to resolve your issues and evaluate the viability of the relationship is an excellent one. However, I have one concern which I consider very significant.

Your perceptions of what happened are very real to you, and your husband's are very real to him. However, it is possible to have an absolute clear and certain perception of something which is totally fallacious. While a normal person does not distort reality the way a psychotic does, one's interpretation of what happened may be distorted; yet the person may be thoroughly convinced of the validity of the interpretation, and that the incident as perceived was factual.

If you are in a sensitive state and someone says or does something which you interpret as negative or hostile, you will not think, "This is what I *think* he said or did," but rather, "This *is* what he said or did." It is possible that the comment or deed was not actually as you perceived it, but to you your perception was a certainty, and you report it as a fact. When you relate this to your therapist, you are not lying, but reporting an interpretation as though it were a fact. Your therapist, even though he/she should be aware of possible distortions in perception, is nevertheless quite apt to take your account as factual. Based upon this, he/she may form opinions about you and your husband that are not in keeping with fact, but only with your *perceptions* of what happened. The same can, of course, be true with your husband's account to his therapist.

What happens is that your perceptions are then reinforced and may become even more resistant to reinterpretation. If after you relate to your therapist, he/she interviews your husband and receives a totally different version of what happened, he/she may not be able to give serious consideration to the alternate version.

Halachah specifies that if a *dayan* (rabbinical judge) has heard the version of one litigant in the absence of another, he is disqualified to serve as a judge on the case. Even though the other litigant may subsequently present his version of the case, the version the judge heard initially may have caused him to form an opinion which cannot be totally undone, and he approaches the case with a bias.

Although therapy is not litigation, the attitude of the therapist in dealing with both partners of a relationship must be fair and unbiased. I therefore suggest that you reverse the order you suggested; i.e., to first see someone together, and after at least some of the major distortions are clarified, you may then decide whether to continue in conjoint therapy or to see therapists individually. The therapist who sees you both together can also assist in deciding if a separation is advisable.

Although I used litigation as an illustration, it is important to remember that a marriage which may be viable should not be looked upon as an adversary procedure. There are no winners versus losers. With a poor decision, everyone is a loser, and with a good decision, everyone is a winner.

Correspondence 7

I am sixteen, a student in a Bais Yaakov school. I have a married older sister and two younger brothers. Our home has always been observant, and to the best of my knowledge, free of any major problems.

About three years ago, my mother began becoming very meticulous about *milchigs* and *fleishigs*. She insisted on purchasing another refrigerator, because some milk might spill, and this might come in contact with something *fleishig*. None of the people we are friendly with have two refrigerators. My father asked our *Rav*, who said that this was not necessary. But my mother insisted, and we had to put a second refrigerator in the basement because there was no room for it in the kitchen.

This was only the beginning. Things began piling up, and I don't remember in what order. For example, if my mother thought I touched a *fleishig* utensil, she would insist that I promptly wash my hands because I might touch something *milchig*. If I dried my hands on a hand towel after a *fleishig* meal, she promptly threw it into the wash because someone might dry their hands on it and eat *milchig*. If she washed the dishes, she would become a nervous wreck, worried that she had not been careful enough. Finally I offered to do the dishes and she was to stay out of the kitchen until everything was put away. You just cannot imagine how absurd things have become.

I pleaded with my father to do something about this, but he says he is helpless. We all know that this is not healthy behavior, but my mother refuses to see a psychiatrist.

I don't think I can continue to take much more of this. I don't mind doing the dishes everyday, but the pressure my mother puts me under is interfering with my schoolwork, and I feel myself becoming very depressed. I could move in with my married sister who lives in another city, but that would leave my father virtually alone, because my younger brothers cannot be of much help. What do you think I should do?

 It seems that your mother has a severe obsessive-compulsive disorder that has expressed itself in the *milchig-fleishig* symptom, but had it not been this, it would have expressed itself in some other way.

As recently as thirty years ago, obsessive-compulsive neurosis was felt to be a psychological problem, with origins in juvenile magical thinking, wherein one thought that by going through some particular ritual, one could undo some harmful things that one had done or wished. Modern psychiatric thought is that obsessive-compulsive neurosis is essentially a biochemical problem, possible to the same chemical imbalances that cause major depressions, and amenable to treatment with anti-depressant medications. The particular expression of the obsessive-compulsive neurosis will vary with an individual's lifestyle and ideas. Thus, a person with religious practices may develop obsessive-compulsive symptoms of a religious nature, while a person who is not religiously oriented may have the same disease but with symptoms of a different content.

One of the most prominent symptoms in this disorder is the inability to feel certain of anything, and the sufferer is plagued with unresolvable doubts about many things.

Having a rabbi explain the halachah to her would not be of much help, because this is not a problem that is amenable to logical argument. If she does value the opinion of a *rav*, he might try to *gently* impress upon her that this is a condition which has nothing to do with observance of halachah, and which requires medical treatment. There is no question that she is suffering enormous torment, and I am certain that she does indeed want help, but she is, for some reason, very resistive. Perhaps she thinks that accepting a psychiatric diagnosis and treatment would stigmatize her as being "crazy."

If you can get a referral to a local psychiatrist who has had experience with obsessive-compulsive patients, he may be able to guide the family in a methodology to overcome her resistance. There are now some very effective medications that can dramatically relieve this condition, and there may be a recovered patient who will be pleased to meet with your mother and describe his/her recovery from this distressful condition.

Insofar as you leaving your home because of the effects of mother's condition upon you, this would indeed appear advisable for your own welfare, but there are two issues to take into consideration. The first is a halachic question of *kibbud av va'eim* (respect of parents), which, while demanding in some respects, may not preclude your taking the necessary steps for your own welfare. While I believe this to be the case, you should refer this to a competent *posek*.

It is particularly important that you consult a *posek* so that you can be assured that the decision you are making is ethically correct. For example, if the right decision is for you to leave, and you do so without the authoritative opinion of a *posek,* you might find yourself plagued by unwarranted guilt feelings for having left home. On the other hand if the decision is for you to remain, the discomforts and stresses will be much more tolerable with the knowledge that what you have done is correct according to halachah.

The second consideration is the point you mentioned about your father being left alone, but you have not mentioned what his attitude is towards your leaving. He may indeed be supportive of this, and may not be as concerned as you are about his weathering the situation alone. If he does object, then it is necessary to understand the reasons for his opposition, and if the decision is nevertheless for you to leave, then an adequate support system must be put in place so that he can cope with the distressful situation.

Finally, if your mother continues to refuse treatment, I think you, your father, and your *rav* should get together with a psychiatrist, and with all the facts on the table, you can come to the best decision possible.

Correspondence 8

Your book *Let Us Make Man* was a great source of inspiration to me when I became observant. You wrote about "joy and self-esteem," and I have also been reading in other books about the concept of *simchah*.

I am not a particularly unhappy person, but I cannot say that I have reached anything approaching euphoria in being *shomer mitzvos*. What's more, I really cannot see that much euphoria among other observant Jews. I have seen some *chassidim* who sing and dance, but I do not get the feeling that their dancing is really an eruption of joy which cannot be contained.

What can I do to achieve more *simchah*?

All the ethical works, from the time of the Talmud to our own time, stress the pivotal role of *simchah* in Jewish life. Indeed, the Torah states that the direst consequences will befall Israel if it fails to serve G-d with *simchah* (*Deuteronomy* 28:47). Perhaps the extraordinary length of our exile is due to this dereliction.

Already in the days of the Talmud, the Sages bewailed the deterioration that had occurred in the spirit of Torah observance, stating that even though Torah study was flourishing more than in the previous generation, the dedication of the earlier generation was lacking, and that "G-d desires the sincerity of the heart" (*Sanhedrin* 106b). We can only imagine the precipitous fall in the spirit of observance of *mitzvos* that has occurred since then.

That *mitzvos* can generate *simchah* is stated clearly in the Scriptures (*Psalms* 19:9), but a necessary precursor to this is the verse that precedes this, "The Torah of G-d is complete, it restores the soul" (*ibid.* 19:8). It is only when we observe *mitzvos* in their completeness, which includes not only the manual performance of the *mitzvah* but the requisite attitude, that will generate *simchah*. It is also evident from this verse that *meshivas nefesh* (restoration of the soul) must precede *mesamchei lev* (gladdening of the heart).

Meshivas nefesh may be thought of as elimination of the negative; i.e., those thoughts and feelings that lead to dejection. The *Rambam* states that the destructive nature of *atzvus* (sadness) is so evident in the Scriptures that it needs no further discussion (*Commentary* on the *Mishnah*, end of *Berachos*). In the Talmud and in the works of *mussar* and *chassidus,* all the misfortunes that have befallen our people, beginning with the Golden Calf and including the tragedy of the Spies in the Desert (*Numbers* 13-14) can be traced to *atzvus.*

One of the prime causes of *atzvus* is dissatisfaction with whatever one has and the insatiable desire for more and more. It has been said that the last of the Ten Commandments, "You shall not covet," is a summation of the first nine. When a person is truly satisfied with what he has, he is not tempted to transgress any of the Ten Commandments. Unhappiness is thus the result of feeling a lack. It is for this reason that the works of *mussar* emphasize the trait of *histapkus*, being content with whatever one has. Obviously, until we emerge from a state of *atzvus*, it is impossible to achieve *simchah*. For most of us it would be less than honest to claim that we are content with whatever we have.

But, we might ask, if one did indeed achieve a state of contentment with one's portion, is it not true that in spiritual matters one should never be content with what one has achieved, and one should always aspire to more learning, more knowledge, and a closer relationship with G-d? Inasmuch as Torah is infinite, one must always feel a lack, and if feeling a lack results in *atzvus*, how can *atzvus* ever be avoided?

The answer is that there is a fundamental difference between the desire for material things versus spiritual. For example, if one desires to own a luxury automobile and one exerts oneself in every possible way to acquire it but is unable to do so, then one's desire remains frustrated. Not only does one lack what one wants, but all the efforts one exerted in order to achieve it are wasted, which only increases the frustration.

It is totally different with pursuit of Torah and *mitzvos*. If a person makes every conceivable effort to achieve a Torah goal, but for whatever reason is unable to do so, it is considered as though he actually achieved it (*Berachos* 6a). For example, if one has made every possible effort to obtain the four species for Succos, and has left no stone unturned, but has not been able to do so, his sincere intent is equal to actual performance of the *mitzvah*, and his efforts have not been in vain at all. This is in sharp contrast to a material goal, where all the efforts to obtain a luxury automobile amount to nothing if that goal is not achieved. The pursuit of Torah is therefore *meshivas nefesh*, restoring the *neshamah* to a state of contentment, whereas similar aspiration for material things leads only to *atzvus*.

Once *atzvus* has been eliminated, one can proceed to *simchah*. Achievement of *simchah* is contingent upon the value one ascribes to Torah and *mitzvos,* as the Psalmist says, "I rejoice over Your works like one who has found a great treasure" (*Psalms* 119:162). Who can deny the thrill one would experience if one were to win a multi-million dollar sweepstake? If we really believe that which we say in our prayers, that Torah and *mitzvos* are more precious than the finest gold (*Psalms* 19:11), then the performance of a *mitzvah* would indeed result in euphoria. If one thinks how many *mitzvos* one does in each day, one can realize that if *mitzvos* were properly valued, one would indeed be euphoric. Unfortunately, we put on our *tefillin* and *tzitzis,* observe the Shabbos, light the candles, say our *berachos,* listen to the shofar, without becoming ecstatically elated. This is not a deficiency in Torah, but in our valuation of Torah.

A second source of *simchah* is when one progresses towards completion of a project. Whether it is something as minor as fitting in another piece of a jigsaw puzzle or something more significant, such as adding another row of bricks to a building, the awareness that one has advanced towards a goal results in a feeling of joy.

Leading a Torah life requires that we believe that we were created for a mission, and that one's *neshamah* descended to the physical world because it is in need of being fulfilled by performance of the *mitzvos.* Thus, every *mitzvah* one does contributes to the completion of the mission, and should therefore result in no less a thrill than when one has progressed towards completion of a material project. If one were indeed aware that each *mitzvah* is another brick in the structure, one would feel joy in its performance.

Is this attainment of *simchah* beyond our reach? To the degree that we can be *samei'ach bechelko,* content with our material possessions, and to the degree that we value the *mitzvos* as precious jewels, and to the degree that we believe that performance of *mitzvos* is the fulfillment of the purpose of our very existence, to that degree we can achieve *simchah.* As long as our performance of *mitzvos* is merely discharging an obligation and being in compliance with the Torah, but without the spirit of the *mitzvos* that should be inherent in the proper attitude towards the Torah and *mitzvos, simchah* will be beyond our reach.

What about the singing and dancing of some people, which appears to be superficial rather than reflecting an intense state of euphoria? There is a valid concept of doing things "as if," in the hope that this will lead to a more genuine experience (*Pesachim* 50b). If one realizes that one is "rehearsing for the real thing," and does not deceive oneself that this behavior is the much sought-after *simchah,* then it may be a helpful step towards the goal. One should not, however, mistake this behavior for the genuine *simchah* .

Our Sages foretold that as we drew closer to the ultimate Redemption, proper fulfillment of Torah and *mitzvos* would become very difficult. Yet, this need not depress us.

The chassidic master, Rabbi Dov Ber of Rodshitz, once lodged at an inn, and in the morning he asked the innkeeper where he had obtained his clock. "Every time the clock chimed the hour, I felt myself drawn out of bed with an urge to dance," he said. The innkeeper told him that this clock had been given to him as a pledge by a descendant of the Seer of Lublin, until he would pay his bill for his lodging.

"Now I understand," Rabbi Dov Ber said. "Usually the chiming of the clock is depressing, because it indicates that another hour of one's life has joined the irretrievable. With the Seer of Lublin, each hour was perceived as one hour closer to the Redemption."

While we share with the Sages of the Talmud the awareness of our imperfection in the spirit of observance of Torah and *mitzvos* , we should strive for whatever we can achieve. When we do so sincerely, G-d completes for us that which is beyond our capability, and this should complement our *simchah* .

Correspondence 9

. . . I am turning to you in desperation to help me out of the terrible depression I am in. I have been reading your book, *Living Each Day*, and I hope you can help.

Until about a year ago, I was happily married, or at least I thought so. We had two children, and while I was not earning a fortune, I was making an adequate living. Our home was *shomer Shabbos* and kosher, and our children were about to be enrolled in an Orthodox day school. Observance of Torah had never been questioned. We did not have any major disagreements, at least not any more than the average couple.

Last year I returned from a two-day business trip to find the house empty. My wife left me a note that she could not put up with me any longer and was suing me for divorce. She emptied every cent from our joint account.

I contacted her parents, who were beside themselves with shock. They had not heard from her and the news hit them like a bolt of lightning. After two weeks of searching, I found that she had moved in with another man, a totally unobservant person. I tried to talk with her, but she will only communicate with me through her attorney, who tells me that she is charging me with having molested the children.

Doctor, this is absolutely insane, the worst nightmare one can imagine. I never touched the children, and it is obvious that this is her way of preventing me from getting the children. There is no purpose in my going to a *bais din*, because she will not respond. I have engaged a lawyer who tells me that this is going to be a nasty battle.

I am totally shattered. I cannot imagine what got into her, and I miss my children terribly. If they remain with her, they will be brought up without any Torah education, since she has completely rejected religion.

I cannot work properly. I cannot eat or sleep. I do not think there is anything left for me in life. What can I do?

Your wife's behavior certainly sounds bizarre, and while I do not mean to pour salt on your wounds, the fact is that I have not heard her version. She may be totally without grounds, yet I have seen cases where a wife repeatedly expressed her dissatisfactions to her husband, but he was completely oblivious to them, so much so that he denied ever hearing them. It is possible for a person to have a psychological deafness and blindness so complete that one does not actually *see* or *hear* that which is presented to him.

While this is a possibility, it is also possible that things are indeed as you describe them. It is not unheard of for such situations to occur with suddenness and unpredictability. One possibility is that your wife may have been harboring conflicting attitudes, and conducted herself according to one standard, until she met a man to whose charms she was vulnerable, and this triggered the emergence of the opposite set of attitudes. Since your wife does not wish to discuss her feelings with you, we may never know what actually happened.

Assuming, for the sake of the discussion, that you were not oblivious to her expressions of dissatisfaction and that she had this sudden, unexplained change of heart, the question is what can you do. The legal issues must be addressed as best as possible, for which you have your attorney. The worst you can do is to deny reality, bitter as it may be. We are a nation that has rebuilt itself after inquisitions, pogroms, and the Holocaust. In all of these we were innocent victims, and we certainly received little sympathy or support from the rest of the world. Other nations would long since have faded into oblivion, but we obstinately fight to survive. Much of modern Israel was built by people who have the identification numbers of Auschwitz tattooed on their forearms. We hurt, we cry, we never forget, but we go on.

If your wife's drastic behavior was groundless, then she is indeed a disturbed young woman. It is possible that she is a victim of an emotional disorder, but you are powerless to do anything about this, since she is not seeking any counseling. The only thing you can concentrate on is saving yourself.

The most painful aspect of this is your being deprived of your children. Assuming her accusations are false, they will nevertheless be used against you, and unless your lawyer can perform miracles, your wife is likely to receive custody of the children.

Your lawyer may be able to obtain a court order that she should submit to a psychiatric evaluation, but I would not hold out hope that this will reveal her to be mentally ill. She is sure to find a psychiatrist whom she will convince that the life she lived with you is too restrictive and oppressive. Although you may be able to get visitation rights, she may be able to convince the court that they must be supervised visitations because of her allegations. If she is given custody, she will be in a position to dictate the children's education, and it is unlikely that you can wield much influence over the children. Any attempt to provide them with Torah values is likely to elicit an opinion from a psychologist that giving the children conflicting ideologies will confuse them, and since the mother has primary custody, her choice of education and training should not be disrupted. One of the most painful things a parent can experience is stated in the Torah: "Your sons and daughters will be surrendered to a foreign nation, and your eyes will pine for them all day, but you will be powerless" (*Deuteronomy* 28:32).

Your focus must be primarily on yourself. You have been dealt a crushing blow which can drain your initiative and desire to function. The internal strength which has enabled our people to survive and flourish after disaster is present in the individual as well. Sympathy will get you nowhere, and while you may be justified in feeling sorry for yourself, nothing constructive results from this.

The sources of strength within you need to be exposed so that you can utilize them. Proper counseling from a competent therapist can accomplish this, and I will be glad to give you several names of therapists in your community. If there are problems in your behavior of which you are unaware and which may have contributed to this scenario, these can be brought out and corrected.

Callous as it may sound, you must stop looking at the past, accept it as a *fait accompli*, and turn your energies towards the future. Dwelling on the past is like struggling in quicksand: it only drags you down more quickly.

Is it possible that one day your wife may have a change of heart and wish to reconcile, or at least allow you to have a voice in your children's upbringing? Everything is possible, but you cannot build on this. You must act according to the reality that exists.

People struck by tragedy may become angry at G-d — Why me? What did I ever do to deserve this? If anyone had the right to ask this question, it is the survivors of the Holocaust. The question is a logical one, but there is no logical answer. Yet, they rolled up their sleeves, and, with their tattooed numbers exposed, went on to rebuild their lives. You must do likewise.

Correspondence 10

I am a yeshiva student, seventeen years old. I have always been the brightest in the class, and I enjoyed my status. I got an enormous thrill out of learning. In the beginning of the semester something happened to me. My mind began to be full of doubts: How do I know all this is true? How do I know there really is a G-d? No one has ever seen Him. Thoughts such as these would bother me and divert my attention from study. I was no longer able to concentrate, and the joy of learning disappeared. Within a short time I was no longer the brightest in the class and this depresses me very much.

I have seriously fallen behind in my studies. I sit with the Gemara (volume of Talmud), but my mind is elsewhere. I have lost the joy in living and have begun to wonder why a person must live altogether.

I have talked with my rabbi about this, and he assures me that by *davening* sincerely and saying extra *Tehillim (Psalms)* and learning *mussar* (ethics), I will overcome this, but it just isn't working. I am going through torture, and no one seems to understand or help.

Since I am unable to fully evaluate your problem by interviewing you in person, I must address several major possibilities.

Firstly, there is a psychological condition whose symptoms are precisely those you describe: unrelenting doubt, inability to concentrate, losing the thrill of whatever one is doing, and questioning the point of living. Although this may appear to be a purely psychological problem, which should be remedied by attitudinal changes and moral support, which is what your *rebbe* recommended, it can also be a condition of biochemical origin, which requires appropriate medication.

We easily assume that disturbances within the body; e.g., physical pain, digestive disturbances, or respiratory problems are due to changes in the body's physiology, which can be corrected by appropriate medication: antibiotics, anti-spasmodics, broncho-dila-tors, etc. For some reason, we do not recognize that the brain is a body organ just like the lungs and liver, and that it, too, can be subject to biochemical changes which interfere with its functioning. One such manifestation of biochemical effect on the brain is the group of symptoms you describe. This may be an obsessive-com-pulsive disorder, and is often relieved by appropriate medication. It is important to consider this possibility, because all the talking and moral support available may be ineffective as long as the biochemi-cal condition is untreated.

The cause of these biochemical changes is unknown, and looking for reasons is futile. Unless treated, the depressing effects of this condition — the inability to learn and falling behind in one's studies — now become factors that aggravate the condition, so that a destructive vicious cycle develops.

I strongly suggest that you consult a competent psychiatrist. A non-psychiatric physician may prescribe a tranquilizer, which at best may give you a few hours of respite but will not correct the biochemical changes. A competent psychiatrist will know what medications to use.

However, inasmuch as it is also possible to have intrusive thoughts in the absence of a biochemical change, let me address that possibility.

Firstly, trying to rid oneself of intrusive thoughts by driving them out of your mind is not only an act of futility, but may be counterproductive. Pushing out interfering thoughts is like pushing against a coiled spring: the harder you push it back, the more force it exerts. Trying to drive out an intrusive thought may cause it to penetrate your mind with greater force. The solution is to leave it alone, and it will eventually go away.

But what if the thought is a sinful one? How can one allow oneself to harbor such thoughts?

Your responsibility is to avoid situations that will stimulate improper thoughts, such as by avoiding looking at, listening to, or reading provocative material.

A chassid once asked his Rebbe what he can do about alien thoughts that disturb his *kavanah* (concentration) during prayer. "Why do you call them alien?" the Rabbi asked. "They are very much your own." If you apply yourself to what you should be doing and avoid potential sources of inappropriate thoughts, then those that do occur will truly be alien. For those thoughts, your rebbe's advice was sound. Do your thing and don't try to battle them.

We believe that every person has a *yetzer hara* (evil inclination) that seeks to destroy him. How such destruction is accomplished is immaterial to the *yetzer hara* as long as the objective is achieved. With some people, the *yetzer hara* can successfully incite them to overt violations of the Torah: stealing, cheating, eating non-kosher food, violating the Shabbos, etc. What is he to do, however, with a young man who devotes himself to Torah study all day? Clearly he will get nowhere if he tries to tell you to steal or violate the Shabbos. The *yetzer hara* is very cunning, however, and finds ways to approach everyone. With someone like yourself, he will intrude an annoying doubt or an improper thought, knowing you will be upset by this and try to drive it away. The *yetzer hara* is well aware of the "coiled spring" phenomenon, and once you begin to play his game, he has you hooked. What he wishes to accomplish is exactly what has happened to you: a preoccupation with intrusive thoughts, distracting you from your studies, and draining your energies, causing you to fall behind and resulting in a depression which further disables you from learning. This in turn causes further depression, and gives rise to a vicious cycle. The *yetzer hara* achieved all this simply by placing an improper thought into your mind, and you unwittingly fell into his trap and played the game which he has thus far been winning.

Doubts about the existence of G-d and all other thoughts which we recognize as improper should be understood to be arrows which the *yetzer hara* is shooting at you. Your reaction should be no different than if he were to tell you to eat *treifah*. It is an absurdity which you simply do not wish to deal with. The important thing is to recognize it as an absurdity which requires no action by you. Simply ignore it and it will eventually go away.

Having said that, we should also be aware that doubts about *emunah* (faith) should not necessarily be considered threatening. *Emunah* is a *mitzvah*, and like any other *mitzvah*, requires energy output to be fulfilled. We must struggle to have proper *emunah*, and this struggle consists of overcoming doubts. Without doubts there may be no true *emunah*.

Let me share with you a thought of Rabbi Yitzchak Meir of Gur. He cited the *Midrash* which states that prior to giving the Torah to the Israelites at Sinai, G-d offered the Torah to various other nations. The Edomites asked, "What does the Torah require?" When G-d responded, "Thou shalt not kill," they rejected the Torah. "Our heritage is to live by the sword," they said. When He offered the Torah to the Ishmalites, they similarly asked what the Torah required, and G-d said, "You shall not commit adultery." "But we are a people of lust," they said. "The Torah is not for us." All nations found reasons to reject the Torah. When He presented the Torah to the Israelites, He began with "I am the L-rd your G-d," and Israel accepted the Torah.

The *Midrash* states that G-d offered the Torah to all other nations so that when, in the World to Come, Israel will be elevated above all other nations, the latter should not be able to claim that G-d is unjust, saying "Had You given the Torah to us, we would have been like Israel." G-d therefore gave them the opportunity to accept the Torah.

The Rabbi of Gur asks, "How does this disarm the other nations? They will still argue, 'You challenged us with restrictions against theft, lust, murder, etc., but to Israel you said "I am your G-d." Why did you not present the content of the Torah equally to all of us?' "

Rabbi Yitzchak Meir explained that the function of the Torah is, as the *Midrash* states, to refine a person's character (*Vayikra Rabbah* 13:3). The challenge of Torah is therefore directed against the most prominent and intense character defects of a nation. Other nations were challenged with their respective character weaknesses: lust, theft, murder, etc. None of these are primary among Jews, whose greatest character deficit is stubborn skepticism, as Moses stated, "They are a stiff-necked people" (*Exodus* 34:9). Idolatrous nations had no difficulty in believing that trees, rivers, and mountains were gods, and readily worshipped their own handcrafted idols as being gods. Israel, however, after witnessing overt miracles in Egypt, the dividing of the Red Sea, the manna, the spring of water that followed them in the desert, the pillars of fire and cloud that guided them through the wilderness, nevertheless remained skeptical, and at every turn, reasserted their doubts as to the presence of G-d among them. Therefore, said the Rabbi of Gur, G-d challenged Israel not with, "Can you restrain your drives towards lust, theft, and murder," but with "I am the L-rd your G-d," in other words, "Can you believe?"

This character defect of skepticism is inherent in Jews, and recurring doubts should not come as a surprise to us. This is a character fault which we must struggle to overcome. Rather than be upset by the presence of such thoughts, those who are *not* bothered by them might have reason for concern. "Am I a true believer? Do I have real *emunah,* or am I just accepting something without a struggle?"

Rabbi Leib Eiger was the son of the great Talmudist Rabbi Shlomo Eiger, who was an ardent opponent of chassidism. Rabbi Shlomo was much grieved when Rabbi Leib became a follower of the Rabbi of Kotzk. After several years, when Rabbi Leib returned home, Rabbi Shlomo asked him, "What did you accomplish in the years you spent in Kotzk?"

"I came to know that G-d runs the world," Rabbi Leib answered.

"And for that you spent all that time?" Rabbi Shlomo asked. He then called in one of the kitchen help, a young woman with no formal education. "Who runs the world?" he asked.

"Why, G-d, of course!" the young woman responded.

Rabbi Leib said to his father, "She *says*, but I *know*."

Achieving *emunah* today is today's *mitzvah*. Tomorrow requires a new assertion of *emunah*, a new struggle. Do not be disillusioned by the ongoing need to reinforce *emunah*, because that is how it is supposed to be.

Elsewhere I described that lobsters grow by shedding their rigid shell when they feel it has become too compressing, and forming a new one. The discomfort the lobster feels is not a negative experience. Quite the contrary, it is a stimulus for additional growth. When you feel yourself doubting, use it as a springboard for a greater *emunah*. You can thereby turn the *yetzer hara's* arrows against him and utilize them for growth in *kedushah*.

Sometimes intrusive thoughts do not involve *emunah*, but are of a lustful character. These arise from basic protoplasmic drives that are present in both man and animals. What distinguishes man from animals is that the latter are dominated by their internal drives and act to satisfy them without delay, whereas a human being can be master over oneself and control one's behavior. There would be no *mitzvah* in restraining oneself from gratifying lust if the latter did not exist. A firm and absolute commitment to resist improper drives eventually results in their attenuation, and when such thoughts arise, have in mind that by not acting upon them you are fulfilling the Divine *mitzvah*. You may ask G-d to relieve these annoying thoughts, since inasmuch as they are part of our animal nature, we cannot extirpate them ourselves. Remember that asking G-d to do something is only a request, and not a command. G-d may wish you to grow in character by persistently struggling to overcome these drives, because spiritual growth cannot occur without struggle.

Had Adam not transgressed with the Tree of Knowledge, the nature of man's service of G-d would have been much easier. Since he did, it is now our struggle, and if you will consult the works of *mussar* and *chassidus*, you will see that this is to be expected. "Man was created to struggle" is how these works interpret the verse in Job (5:7). Each day you successfully emerge from the struggle is a day of accomplishment of your ultimate goal. Although you may be disappointed that you did not achieve as much study of Torah as you wished on that day, do not let this depress you. Your day has been a successful one, albeit it was one of much stress.

We must make an effort to study Torah even if we do not feel ourselves ideally disposed to do so, because being in distress is not an exemption to the *mitzvah* of Torah study. Be assured that you will again achieve the thrill and joy of learning.

Correspondence 11

 . . . I am now twenty-two, and although I am not an old maid, I feel left out as many of my friends are engaged or married. I do not think I am unattractive, and although I have had dates which seemed to have promise, nothing ever developed into a serious relationship.

I consulted a psychologist, and I told him that I felt my problem is one of low self-esteem. I read your book, *Let Us Make Man*, and I was able to see myself in many of the examples you described as being due to low self-esteem.

I live in an Eastern Seaboard city, and after finishing school in New York, I returned home. I live with my parents and have a good job with a large firm.

Although I am not a Bais Yaakov graduate, many of the girls in my school, as well as I, believe in the prohibition of refraining from physical contact with men. When I told this to my psychologist, he told me that my problem was not low self-esteem but that I had set up an unrealistic barrier to a relationship. This does not make much sense, since it does not appear to prevent my friends from developing successful relationships. I discontinued seeing him after several sessions.

There are no Orthodox psychiatrists in my area, and it is unrealistic for me to go to New York. What do you suggest?

It is unfortunate that you hit upon a psychologist who is so short-sighted. Since he is apparently making a living in a community which is not composed of Torah-observant Jews, he must have a clientele who are not subject to Torah restrictions. Since they are not limited to the restrictions you have, why are they having any emotional problems at all that lead them to seek psychologic treatment?

Some 2,500 years ago, there was a famous physician of antiquity, Hippocrates. At that time, epilepsy was considered to be an illness of supernatural origin. Some people believed that it was supernaturally good, and that the seizure was the result of a prophetic vision, while others believed it to be supernaturally bad, and that the person was possessed by a demon or an evil spirit. Hippocrates writes that he dissected the brains of epileptics and found that the brain was diseased. He states that anyone who would examine the brain would conclude that it is a disease that causes the seizure and not a supernatural force.

Hippocrates continues with words that should be taken to heart by every physician and therapist. He states that those who attribute the seizure to G-d or a demon do so because of their impotence in treating the disease, and rather than admit that they do not know how to treat it, they blame a supernatural force.

There are still residuals of the psychotherapeutic approach that seek to place blame of a person's difficulties on one's parents. While there is no denying that the parental influence on the child is considerable and it may help for the patient to understand some of the dynamics of the symptoms, the practice of scapegoating parents is of little value and is to be deplored. People have lost valuable relationships because therapists drove wedges between parents and children. The reason for this practice is no different than that cited by Hippocrates: an effort to divert attention from the limitations of therapy (or the therapist) by scapegoating the parents. Your psychologist apparently chose to scapegoat religion rather than to seek to help you with your problem.

One important factor that you did not address is your living in a city where there is not a large Orthodox community, therefore your contacts with young men of the orientation you seek must be rather limited. You might consider finding a job in a large urban community, such as New York, where your contacts would be more extensive.

Insofar as therapy is concerned, you should be able to avail yourself of a therapist who does not project the problem to religious restrictions. There are now many therapists who do not ascribe to Freud's theory which considered all religion as neurotic, and who will respect the client's right to behave according to one's belief.

I am pleased that you are aware that you are attractive, because people with low self-esteem are fully capable of denying their own reality, and I know of handsome people who have thought themselves to be homely and of exceedingly bright people who considered themselves to be dull. One woman who was a superior person in many ways but had a very poor self-concept, considered herself to be very boring. When I confronted her with the fact that she had won the coveted Phi Beta Kappa Award for scholastic excellence in college, her response was, "When they told me I had won the Phi Beta Kappa Award I knew they had made a mistake."

While you may feel secure in your physical appearance, you may nevertheless be harboring gross distortions about your personality. One of my colleagues, a highly respected internal medicine specialist, spends all his waking hours a the hospital and office, and his teaching activities and dedication to his patients have endeared him to his students, staff and patients. His late hours at the hospital led some people to conclude that his wife must be a very difficult person to live with, hence he spends much time at the hospital in order to avoid her.

The doctor's wife consulted me when she became depressed, and I was rather surprised to meet a very gentle, considerate, and loving person. She said, "You know how dedicated my husband is to his work. I am a very needy and insecure person, and I needed a shoulder on which to rest my head, but he was never there for that. Our children grew up without a father, because although he treated them when they were sick, he was never there to listen to them or to guide them."

What happened with this doctor was that his self-esteem was dichotomized. He recognized his excellence as a physician, but was unaware that he was also a very fine and gifted *person*. Hence he was comfortable at the hospital, for which he felt qualified, but not at home where he felt that as a *person* he had nothing to contribute.

Just as you are aware of being physically attractive, you must also become aware of your personality assets. You do not suspect the mirror of lying to you when it compliments you on your image, and you must also be able to accept the assessment of an objective observer when he/she assures you of your personality strengths.

The fact that your dates "seem to have promise" indicates that the initial impression others have of you is positive. If these relationships subsequently fail to thrive it is undoubtedly due to something you inadvertently do to bring this about, but the initial favorable impression attests that you have personality assets that make you desirable.

If you feel comfortable taking your local rabbi into your confidence, you may find that he has had contact with local therapists whom he can recommend. If you do not wish to do so, I will be glad to make some inquiries for you to locate a therapist who is qualified in self-esteem problems and bears no antagonism towards religion.

At twenty-two, there is certainly no grounds for panic, even though many of your peers are already married. Since I believe low self-esteem to be at the root of most problems, and to some degree as present in people who have not identified any specific symptoms, I am sure that correcting your self-image will remove the barriers to your forming the relationship(s) you seek.

Correspondence 12

. . . Today I discovered a letter I wrote four months ago. Obviously I forgot to mail it, and I had assumed you were too busy to answer. As I reread the letter, I realized that I have a bit of different perspective now.

I am married five years and we have three children. My husband and I, although both from *frum* homes, are as different as can be. We have no common interests and nothing to share. What is infinitely worse is that he is a very controlling person, and I am putty in his hands. He has no idea that he is emotionally abusive. If he had struck me, he might be aware of his abusiveness. When I wrote you initially I was looking for a way to leave the marriage. I am here in Israel all alone, and my entire family is in the U.S. My husband would be furious if he knew I were thinking in these terms. At that time I was desperate, but I have now found a therapist whom I have seen several times without my husband's knowledge. My husband is a prominent person in the religious community and would never agree with this.

The situation has essentially not changed, but I am not as desperate as I was. I still do not believe the marriage can continue, but I do not feel that I must get out right now. I would still like your opinion.

I am pleased that you have begun to see a therapist, because there are a number of issues that require clarification.

Since you both come from observant families and have remained observant, it is quite incorrect that you do not share any common interests. Shabbos, Passover, Succos, Shevuous, Chanukah, Purim, are common interests. Giving the children a Torah education is a common interest, as are all the other observances and values you share. You may not share other interests, such as drama, music, and literature, but if these things and the like are the major points of difference, then they may have assumed a disproportionately great significance in your life. I do not minimize other interests that you would like to share, but I suspect that their importance may be exaggerated.

What is of greater concern is that you describe your husband as controlling and emotionally abusive. I do not doubt that he is totally unaware of this. Some husbands have a paternalistic attitude and treat their wives as though they were juveniles. They actually feel they are looking after their best interests, and they may be unaware that this attitude is demeaning, and that the wife is a mature person who can take care of herself and make her own decisions.

For such a situation to exist requires the participation of both partners, one who controls and the other who allows oneself to be controlled. I do not mean to blame the victim, but it is really impossible to have a controlling situation when one does not allow oneself to be controlled.

Much of my writing has been on issues of self-esteem. I have differentiated healthy self-effacement (*anivus*) from pathological self-effacement resulting from a person's unwarranted feelings of inadequacy and unworthiness. The latter is prone to result in passivity, which then brings along with it the anger and resentment at being manipulated. In my book *Like Yourself and Others Will Too* (Prentice-Hall, 1978), I wrote that "If you will be a doormat, people will wipe their feet on you." Only you yourself can define yourself as a doormat.

It is important that you consider the self-esteem issues in therapy, and develop your self-esteem to the point where you will not allow yourself to be a passive victim. Although this may not be an abrupt change, it is possible that it may elicit a critical response from your husband. I recall the case of a woman who recovered from severe agoraphobia (fear of public places and crowds) and her husband was bitterly disappointed that she no longer had to rely on him to go anywhere. Your husband may need some enlightenment on the changes that will be taking place in you.

You state that your husband will react violently to your being in therapy. You have to discuss just how and when to handle this problem with your therapist. It is inconceivable for a marriage to proceed happily when one spouse is concealing something so important. This revelation does not have to come about at this very moment, but it cannot be delayed forever. When your husband is apprised of the changes in you and that you are involved in therapy, he may change his mind and choose to participate. If he does not, then this too must be handled in therapy.

The crucial factor is to work with your therapist in building self-esteem. With self-esteem, whatever course you take can be constructive. Without self-esteem, any adjustment you make cannot be satisfactory over the long term.

Correspondence 13

 ... I have read some of what you have written about low self-esteem, and I felt as though you were writing about me.

I am twenty-eight, a former yeshiva student, employed, and I had hoped by now to have been married. However, I seem to strike out on every date. Each time I am rejected, it makes me feel even less self-confident.

I know this did not start now, because I have been very shy and withdrawn all my life, even as a child. I am one of three children, and my older sister and younger brother are married. My home was a fairly normal one, and I cannot attribute the way I feel about myself to anything specific. What do you suggest I do?

My purpose in writing about problems of low self-esteem was not to provide a cookbook containing recipes for recovery, but rather to help people recognize what the problem is so that they may seek the proper help. In this sense, the fact that you have identified the problem is an important step in the right direction. Many people develop defensive patterns, especially projecting blame for any failures in life onto everyone else, and do not even consider that they must do something to correct their own attitude.

I have tried in my writings, especially in *Let Us Make Man,* to give some basic principles on why a person should have a positive attitude about himself, and for those people who are students of *mussar* (ethics), to be cautious not to confuse positive self-esteem with *gahvah* (vanity). Whereas humility is an important virtuous character trait, it should not be confused with low self-esteem. Humility is positive and constructive, whereas low self-esteem is a distortion of one's self concept, and thus is negative and destructive.

Your particular case reminds me of a young man who consulted me for a psychological problem. In relating his history, he incidentally stated that he had no luck whatever in establishing a romantic relationship, being rejected after every date. Then his best friend, who was being sent off to Vietnam, asked him to please provide occasional companionship for his fiance during his absence. He did so, and the young woman fell in love with him.

What had happened was that because this young man had a poor self-image, he was certain that if a young woman would see him as he really was, she would certainly not be attracted to him. He therefore tried to present himself in a better light, and because he was tense and under stress to make a good impression, this strategy caused him to behave in an artificial, awkward fashion that precluded the possibility of attraction. When he related to his friend's fiance, however, he had no interest whatever of impressing her, since he was simply trying to do his buddy a favor of providing some friendly companionship for her. He behaved spontaneously, in a relaxed manner, and was just himself, which allowed the young woman to see the real person, with whom she fell in love. In other words, trying too hard can backfire. Perhaps if you could relax when meeting a young woman, you would be pleasantly surprised.

However, in order to be relaxed and be oneself while trying to make a favorable impression, you must feel good about yourself, which has obviously not been the case since your childhood.

Reading appropriate books on self-esteem may be of some help, but usually falls short of doing the job. As I pointed out, my writings are primarily to help a person realize that the problem is a distortion of the self-image. Many people are adamant that their self-perception is not distorted, and that they are indeed inadequate in various ways. This self-perception is a delusion no less than is a delusion of the paranoid who believes grandiose things about himself and cannot be swayed by any logical argument to consider that he might be mistaken. I hope that my writings can, at the very least, help a person realize that regardless of how certain one feels that one has an accurate self-knowledge, one should consider the possibility that one's self-perception may be incorrect.

Correction of the self-image often requires professional attention, and the help of a competent psychologist should be sought. There has been some resistance among Torah-observant people to seek psychological counseling or therapy, because they see this as a threat to their *Yiddishkeit*. This undoubtedly had its origin in the days when Freudian theory dominated the field, and many psychotherapists who were loyal to Freudian principles believed that religious observance was a neurosis, and that the various restrictions imposed by religion were oppressive and thus a cause of the individual's emotional problems. It should have been obvious to them that people who are totally free of any religious commitment and who have no restrictions on their behavior have at least as many, if not more emotional problems.

In the past several decades there has been a major shift in psychological thinking. Many conditions, such as some types of depression, phobias, panic, and obsessive-compulsive disorders are felt to be primarily biochemical in origin. Psychotherapy has become much more behavior-oriented, directed towards correcting what one is doing, rather than searching for the roots of one's behavior. Many psychologists do not harbor any antagonism towards religion.

Some people, however, are under the impression that an emotional problem cannot be resolved unless one gets to the root of the problem. This is not necessarily so. Particularly when one has a problem of low self-esteem, it is not essential to know how and why the distortion of the self-concept came to be, but rather to correct the self-perception and enable the person to see the real self.

The medical therapeutic approach is understandably to find the source of the patient's pain or discomfort: the infection, tumor, fracture, or hormonal imbalance. In problems of low self-esteem, it may actually be counterproductive to search for what is *wrong* with the patient, but rather to help him see what is *right* about him. The patient already knows enough about what is wrong with him. Indeed, he knows many "wrongs" that exist nowhere except in his imagination. A therapeutic approach that is based on the medical model, while perhaps appropriate for some psychological problems, may not be appropriate for self-esteem problems. It is therefore necessary to enlist the help of a psychotherapist who is not oriented toward looking for the pathology, but for discovering a person's strengths.

I am not familiar with any psychotherapists in your community, hence I cannot make a referral. You might do some research on your own, perhaps consulting a local rabbi or a friend who has had contact or is knowledgeable about psychotherapists in your area. In the absence of such referral sources, I would suggest asking for a psychologist who is trained in "cognitive therapy." In my opinion, this school, as a rule, has the desirable orientation for resolving low self-esteem problems.

A person is required by halachah to seek competent medical treatment for a disease, and while praying for Divine help is important, and receiving *berachos* (blessings) from *tzadikkim* (pious people) is encouraged, the rule of וּבֵרַכְתִּיךָ בְּכֹל מַעֲשֵׂי יָדְךָ אֲשֶׁר תַּעֲשֶׂה, "I will bless you in everything that you do," applies to diseases as well. One must do whatever is medically advisable while praying for a *refuah* (cure). This holds true for psychological problems as well.

In this vein, it is notable that Rabbi Yerucham, one of the foremost Jewish ethicists, states that Divine help is necessary to emerge from low self-esteem. Rabbi Yerucham comments on the verse, דָּחֹה דְחִיתַנִי לִנְפֹּל וַה׳ עֲזָרָנִי — "They pushed me hard that I might fall but G-d helped me" (*Psalms* 118:13) that within *every* person there is a force that operates to crush him, and that one must appeal for Divine help to avoid succumbing to this force. The widespread occurrence of low self-esteem may therefore be due to this crushing force, which Rabbi Yerucham states is universal, inherent in *every* individual, and against which one must struggle just as one must struggle against all destructive internal drives.

"The praise of G-d is in their throats and the sharp sword in their hand" (*Psalms* 149:6). Just as one wages battle against an enemy with a combination of weapons and prayer, so one must battle destructive psychologic forces with both appropriate therapy and prayer.

Correspondence 14

I am nineteen, and learning in a yeshiva. During the past two summers I worked in a camp for children with various psychologic problems, such as mental retardation and autism. I seem to have a way with these children. They relate to me, and I enjoy working with them and maximizing each child's potential.

I am thinking of going to college for a degree in educational psychology, but to really do this would occupy most of my time for the next seven years. I could be devoting this time to Torah, and to go for a degree in psychology would be a major commitment.

As both a rabbi and a psychiatrist I am asking your advice.

I am glad you qualified your question as seeking advice rather than a rabbinic decision, for which you must consult a *posek* (halachic authority). I wish to elaborate a bit on this point.

Some people, because they have had a yeshiva education and they have even obtained *semichah* (rabbinic ordination) consider themselves qualified to make halachic decisions, at least for themselves. They may be professionals or businessmen who continue their daily Torah study.

Rendering a halachic decision requires a special mind-set. People who are primarily occupied with business or professions have a business or professional mind-set, which is not conducive to making halachic decisions. It is well known that some of the greatest Torah scholars, who were deans of *yeshivos*, refrained from rendering halachic decisions, and referred all such questions to the local *posek*. While their Torah knowledge was immense, and may have even been greater than that of the *posek*, they felt that they did not have the mind-set necessary for a halachic decision. I can thus give you an opinion, but only an opinion.

The problem of children who have mental and emotional problems has only rather recently begun to receive attention in the Torah community. Unfortunately, some families, worried that exposure of a mental problem in the family will jeopardize *shidduchim* (matrimonial matches) for their other children, may try to conceal the problem rather than obtain the proper help.

While children with mental and emotional limitations may not be able to achieve the level of learning and skills of normal children, it is a gross injustice to fail to maximize those skills they do possess. Many of them are educable, and there are techniques that can develop their potential.

Many educators are people who like to see major progress resulting from their efforts. It is a thrill to see a child learn how to read, write and do arithmetic. It is most gratifying to have students who learn Torah well and understand Talmudic discourses.

I once visited an abandoned gold mine, and the guide told me that there is still a great deal of gold in the mine, but it is so diluted with other substances that the effort and cost needed to extract it would not be justified by the amount of gold obtained. Miners of gold work with ore whose percentage of gold content warrants time and energy expended.

While such thinking can apply commercially, it should not apply to a child with mental limitations. Every bit of potential should be brought to fulfillment. If most educators have a need to see kilograms of gold resulting from their work and are not satisfied with milligrams, then the one who is able to be satisfied with milligrams is a rare resource who should be exploited.

If G-d has given you the skills and personality that enable you to relate to these children and to be gratified by maximizing their potential even if they cannot be high performers, it is my opinion that you have a responsibility to capitalize on these talents for the benefit of such children who might otherwise be neglected. There are specialized courses which teach various techniques and methodologies to enhance your innate skills.

What about your personal learning of Torah? Will that not suffer if you spend so much of your time in specialized educational psychology?

I can only tell you what one *gadol* (Torah authority) told me when I went into psychiatry. I, too, noted that the training for and practice of psychiatry would deter me from being totally devoted to Torah study. In those days, psychiatry was heavily under the influence of Freudian theory, and Torah-observant people were hesitant to consult a psychiatrist who might challenge their Torah orientation. The *gadol* told me that a *mitzvah* which cannot be performed by anyone else overrides the *mitzvah* of the study of Torah.

Please remember, this is an opinion, and not a halachic decision.

Correspondence 15

I am a rabbi, thirty-three, and in the past five years since receiving my *semichah* (ordination), I have held three positions. I left the first two under somewhat similar circumstances, and the same pattern has now begun to manifest itself in this position.

Strangely, my class had voted me the most likely to succeed. I was always at the head of my class in yeshivah, and I have achieved some recognition from *poskim* (halachic authorities) with whom I have consulted on various *sh'eilos* (halachic questions). I am told that my *derashos* (sermons) are marvelous.

I think that what happened in my first two positions was simply a result of personality clashes, particularly because I was inexperienced in dealing with people. Yeshivah gave me a fine background in halachah, but nothing in interpersonal relationships. I do not see any need for implicating any psychopathology on my part, but my wife says that she sees a repetition of a pattern for the third time, and is concerned that if I develop a negative reputation, my future as a rabbi will be undermined in spite of my academic qualifications.

Initially I am received enthusiastically, and the first few months are a honeymoon period. I assume that since you were once a pulpit rabbi yourself, you are aware that in any shul some differences of opinion arise. In the first instance it began with a member of the shul who married a non-Jewish woman who did not convert. He continued to come to shul as though nothing had occurred, attending the Talmud *shiur* (class), etc. While I did not insist on his being expelled, I took a firm position that he could not have an *aliyah* (being called to the reading of the Torah) or *hakafah* (carrying the Torah in procession), and the overwhelming body of the membership supported me. One influential member, who also was in favor of my stand, suggested that I handle things with a bit more diplomacy and tact. I disagreed with him, and from there on I began having difficulty with him and a powerful faction in the shul, which eventually escalated to the point where I exerted my authority and publicly rebuked him. In retrospect, perhaps I was overreacting, but it concluded with my having to leave.

In my second position the story was almost identical, except for the triggering incident of disagreement. As rabbi of the shul I was on the advisory board of the local day school. There were a few children from non-observant homes, and on school outings, they would bring obviously *treife* (non-kosher) lunches. Again I was supported in the firm stand I took, that while we could not control what happened in students' homes, we could not tolerate *treife* food at a school event, even if it were held not on the school grounds. Again I was urged to handle the matter with greater finesse, and when my methodology was attacked, I counterattacked with vigor, and again the problem escalated to an explosive state.

I am now in my third position, and my wife says she can see the germination of another blowup. During the Gulf War, the only child of one of the officers in the navy was bar mitzvah, and the father could not get leave to attend the event. They are not an observant family, but for several generations their family has belonged to our shul, and they are loyal members. They asked to have the bar mitzvah videotaped on Shabbos by non-Jews, so that the father could see the bar mitzvah. While I certainly sympathized with the family, I took the position that we could not permit videotaping in shul on Shabbos, even by a non-Jew. Again, the membership is in agreement with me, but some members of this influential family are leaving the shul. My wife fears that I will "mishandle" this as I have the first two, which, incidentally, I do not think I mishandled.

Perhaps my solution is to take a position in a shul which is solidly Torah-observant, where such conflicts will not occur. My wife says I will be running away from a psychological problem that I need to resolve, and that unless I do so, problems will occur regardless of the orientation of the shul.

I am familiar with you through your books, and I have attended some of your lectures. As both a rabbi and a psychiatrist, what is your opinion?

 As you know, there is a halachic argument whether a pattern is established by two similar occurrences or three. Certainly in the cases the Talmud considers, factors could be found in each case to consider them *dis*similar, and hence that they do not constitute a pattern. Yet, the individual factors are disregarded, and the assumption is that there is a pattern. While the final halachah is that it takes three incidents to establish a pattern, there is an opinion that when it is a question of life and death, one should be cautious and assume that even two similar incidents constitute a pattern. Your reputation may well be of the magnitude of a "life or death" issue, and you might therefore consider that two incidents constitute a pattern. There are sufficient grounds to, at the very least, pursue a further evaluation.

Having been a pulpit rabbi, I can certainly identify with you. However, in my work in psychiatry, I have become convinced that whenever any adjustment problems exist, particularly of an interpersonal nature, they can invariably be traced to an underlying feeling of low self-esteem. It appears that on two occasions you were told that you were absolutely right, and that while everyone agreed with your goals, there was a question of methodology. In both cases you chose a methodology which, it appears, was provocative.

In my writings on self-esteem, I pointed out that people who are particularly gifted may actually have a lower self-concept than people who are objectively far inferior to them. Your demonstrated excellence thus, by no means, rules out an underlying low self-esteem. Indeed, a person is sometimes stimulated to over-achievement in order to compensate for a gnawing feeling of inadequacy and unworthiness.

In my book *Like Yourself and Others Will Too* (Prentice-Hall, 1978), I described the case of a young man who was terribly frightened that he would be rejected in a romantic relationship, and the tension of anticipating the eventual rejection, which he felt was inevitable, became so unbearable that in order to escape the tension he precipitated the rejection, simply to get it over and done with.

While I do not have adequate grounds to state that this is operative in your case, the vibrations I pick up in your letter make me think that this is a possibility. The importance of considering this is that if this is indeed so, then accepting a position in an ultra-Orthodox shul, where there will be no major halachic issues, will not prevent a re-occurrence.

In other words, if you harbor an unconscious attitude, for example, that you are not really likable or desirable, and you have an underlying feeling that it is only a matter of time before you will be rejected, it is very possible that you may initiate those actions that will result in your being rejected. This is not a consciously planned maneuver, and you may be totally unaware that you are doing it or why you are doing it. In fact, you may have excellent explanations of why you are acting in a particular way, and you may be thoroughly convinced that you are justified in doing so.

I have seen people go from job to job, change careers, break up marriages, and even after all of the above, are totally unaware that they are reacting out of an unwarranted low self-esteem. In each situation they present abundant reasons to justify what they are doing, and give convincing accounts of how they are the innocent victims of other people's obstinacy. I have seen two people confronted with essentially the same situation react in totally different fashion, one with a favorable outcome, and the other with an unfavorable outcome, and I have been able to correlate their respective reactions with their sense of self-esteem.

A person with the demonstrated intellect and skills that you possess is not likely to be devoid of tact and diplomacy, and I would not attribute the unfavorable results in your first two positions to such a lack. I strongly suggest that you avail yourself of an evaluation by someone qualified in self-esteem problems, and I would be glad to provide you with names of people you may consult.

Correspondence 16

I know you have heard this before. I have recently begun to drink, but I don't believe I am an alcoholic. I am thirty-four, married to a wonderful man and we have three children. But my husband, who is truly a wonderful man, cannot detach himself from his mother. He has two brothers, but he is the only one upon whom his mother calls for everything. On his one day away from the office, when he should be with me and the children, his mother will call for him to cut her grass and do other chores around the house, and he promptly responds. Some of these things are trivial, and I have the feeling she does this simply to take him away from us. When we wish to go out to dinner as a family, we invite her to come along. When she refuses, as she usually does, my husband will not take us unless she changes her mind.

I believe my husband loves me, but he claims that he is obligated by the Torah to honor his mother. I felt trapped and began to drink to relieve my anger at him and her, as well as to mitigate my severe frustration. I feel that if he would give me and the children the attention we are entitled to, I would not need to drink.

Do you think I am an alcoholic?

On the basis of the information you have provided, I cannot make a diagnosis. Many alcoholics can give perfectly logical reasons for their excessive drinking, but are nevertheless alcoholic. Sometimes there may be an apparent reason why the drinking began, but the drinking may continue even after the reason is no longer present. I would suggest you avail yourself of a thorough evaluation by someone competent in alcohol problems to arrive at a correct diagnosis.

Totally separate from your question about alcoholism is your husband's behavior. Inasmuch as he is invoking a halachic reason for his relationship to his mother, it is important that he consult a competent halachic authority to find out precisely what halachah does specify in such a situation. *Kibbud av va'eim,* honoring one's parents, is considered one of the foremost *mitzvos,* and the *Midrash* equates honoring one's parents with honoring G-d Himself. Yet, like all other *mitzvos,* there are regulations governing its performance, and these are found in the Talmud and *Shulchan Aruch.*

The very same Torah that requires honoring one's parents also says, "Therefore a man shall leave his father and mother and cleave unto his wife" (*Genesis* 2:24). What does one do when these two appear to conflict? One consults a competent halachic authority. Behavior of the Torah-observant Jew should be governed by halachah rather than by emotion.

Emotions are unreliable guides to action, and are likely to distort one's logic, resulting in abnormal behavior. While the latter may often be recognized as abnormal, it is more difficult to do so when it takes on a religious flavor, because one can then claim that one is acting according to strict requirements of the law. It is therefore necessary to consult a halachic authority to determine what it is that Torah requires.

For example, most people who prepare their homes for Passover have a secluded corner where they retain *chametz* to be eaten until the designated time on the day before Passover. Some people who are concerned that they may not be able to get rid of all the *chametz* will avoid bringing *chametz* into the home for several days prior to Passover. However, I had one patient who refused to allow *chametz* into her home all year for fear that she might not be able to clean adequately for Passover. It does not take much to realize that this woman had an emotional problem resulting in behavior that was grossly absurd, and could in no way be ascribed to even the most exacting halachic requirements. While the absurdity in the example cited is evident, there are lesser degrees of distortion that may not be as easily recognizable.

Rabbi Levi Yitzchak of Berdichev said that inasmuch as the violation of Shabbos is a grave sin and there are so many things that one may inadvertently do that would transgress Shabbos, the only way one could be absolute certain not to violate Shabbos was to have oneself tied securely in a chair from the time of sunset Friday to Saturday night. However, if one did so, this would constitute the gravest violation of Shabbos, which is supposed to be a day of *oneg* (pleasantness), and not a day of misery.

Wherever protective regulations were necessary to avoid transgressing the Torah, our Sages provided them, and these constitute the various *gezeiros* (rabbinical decrees). We need not add to these.

Your husband has two brothers who should participate in assisting their mother. If she chooses to place the entire responsibility only on him, it is questionable whether he is required to comply. Furthermore, the halachah in the *Shulchan Aruch* and the responsa provides regulations for the *mitzvah* of *kibbud av va'eim*. Some children relate to their parents out of a sense of guilt, which is not only a very unreliable guide, but also results in their relating to their parents with feelings of resentment for being burdened with their care. Performance of *mitzvos* should not be done with or result in resentment. Following halachic guidelines will result in appropriate respect for parents, while permitting devotion to one's family and a positive, pleasant, and joyous attitude, rather than one of guilt and resentment.

Correspondence 17

. . . I am a *kollel* wife, and I should be happy, but I am not.

I've been married for five years and we have three children. My husband is a fine *talmid chacham* (Torah scholar) and helps me with the children to the best of his ability. Our parents help us financially, and while we are not destitute, we do have to count our pennies. There are some *kollel* families who come from wealthy backgrounds, and they do have nice cars and can afford vacations, but I don't think that bothers me. I do not feel envious of them.

For the first two years of our marriage we lived in tiny quarters, and when our second child arrived, we moved to a very comfortable apartment. Some time after that is when I really began to feel unhappy. I am functioning normally in every way, but just without *cheshek* (enthusiasm).

I don't remember being unhappy as a child. I received a Bais Yaakov education, and I looked forward to marrying a *talmid chacham* and having the kind of lifestyle I am living. I am not really worried about the future. My husband is a capable person, and he plans to go into *chinuch* (education) after *kollel,* and I know he will succeed.

I don't know what it is that is making me unhappy now. Sometimes I feel sorry for my husband that he is stuck with me. I give myself totally to my children, but I feel they are not getting much of anything . . .

 Before addressing what I think may be the problem, I wish to alert you to the fact that some depressions are not due to psychological factors, but to subtle chemical imbalances that produce various depressive symptoms. This chemical imbalance may occur secondary to physical causes such as viruses, surgery, or the hormonal changes of menopause, premenstrual phase, or following the birth of a child, or may come out of the blue with no apparent cause. In either case, psychotherapy cannot be effective until the chemical imbalance is corrected by appropriate anti-depressant medication.

Insofar as the psychological problem is concerned, the pattern you describe is not an unusual one. You are doubly fortunate in (1) recognizing that something is wrong, and (2) doing so at an early age. Some people go through an entire lifetime without being aware of a problem, and others discover it at a much advanced stage, having suffered unnecessarily.

In my book, *Like Yourself and Others Will Too*, I discussed a syndrome wherein people who are dissatisfied repeatedly look for reasons to explain their discontent, and anticipate that when the particular factor they have identified as causative is resolved, their uneasiness will disappear. There are enough factors in one's life that one can invariably find something to blame for one's disgruntlement. When all possible factors are exhausted and the discontent nevertheless persists, one then comes face to face with the underlying problem that has been existing for five or six decades but went unattended.

This discontent is most often due to feelings of inadequacy or poor self-esteem that have no factual basis, and are the result of a distorted self-perception that usually begins in childhood (see Chapters 1-7). Once this distorted self-perception takes root, the person may then function accordingly, which often results in reinforcement and aggravation of the low self-esteem. People are generally not aware that this is the reason for their unhappiness, and instead attribute the latter to any one of many causes, and look forward to the time when things will be better, and they will then be happy.

I suspect that during your youth you had a low self-esteem, which you may recognize in retrospect, especially if you learn its symptoms. You may have thought that when you will marry, have a fine husband, a Torah home, healthy children, and be relatively free of financial worries, you will then be happy. Many people function only by anticipation.

You have now come to realize that you essentially have achieved all that you had hoped, but you are not yet happy. I said that you are fortunate, because you might have attributed your unhappiness to not owning your own home, not having a luxury automobile, or any one of many things. You might then have driven your husband to earn more, and the lack of adequate money (which is highly relative) would have served as an explanation for your discontent for many years.

Your low self-esteem is evidenced by your feeling sorry for your husband for having you as a wife, and that regardless of how much you give of yourself to your children, you still are giving them nothing. Your husband has a fine wife, and the children have a fine mother. They know it, but you don't. Furthermore, the nature of low self-esteem is such that regardless of how often you are reassured that you are loved, competent, and adequate, you cannot accept it. It is only after you shed the feelings of inadequacy and begin to believe in yourself, that your discontent will be relieved.

Appropriate psychotherapy can help you overcome this distorted self-perception. Inasmuch as it probably had its onset in your childhood, and you may have unwittingly reinforced it by basing your behavior on this distorted self-perception for twenty plus years, it is not going to be undone in one or two months of therapy.

You should be aware that you will not be consulting a psychologist because there is something "wrong" with you, but to the contrary, because you are unaware of how much there is "right" with you. I therefore believe that you should consult a psychotherapist who is oriented toward helping people discover their true selves and develop a correct self-perception. Some therapists may have an approach of looking for the pathology or for the incident in one's early life that caused the problem. I do not feel this method is effective in self-esteem problems. If you wish, I will be glad to provide you with referrals to several psychotherapists in your area.

There is every reason for optimism that you will achieve a correct self-awareness and a truly happy life.

Correspondence 18

 . . . I was a psychology major in college, and I am aware that a little knowledge may be worse than none, and so I am asking your professional opinion.

I am now 34, and I married at 22. My wife is a child of survivors of the Holocaust, whereas my grandparents came to the U.S. in the 1920s. I had no idea what an impact this difference could make.

I spent three years in *kollel* and received *semichah* (ordination). I am employed as an accountant, and I make a reasonable living. My father-in-law must have been about twelve years old when the war broke out, and he had no opportunity to learn Torah. When he came to the U.S. after the war, he had to spend his entire time trying to earn a living. It is not his fault that he is not a *talmid chacham* (Torah scholar). He knows nothing more than *chumash* with *Rashi* (the Pentetuach with Rashi commentary), although he thinks he does. I fortunately had the opportunity to learn, and I have some degree of Torah scholarship.

My in-laws lost most of their family in the Holocaust. This has caused them to be very possessive of their children, whom they will not leave out of their sight. I am certain that they have many deep emotional scars as a result of the hell they went through.

What I did not realize is that they have an attitude that because they suffered so terribly, they are the elite of the Jewish nation, and anyone who did not suffer along with them is simply unworthy. My parents have no value to them and neither do I. They berate me at every opportunity. The intense closeness of my wife to her parents has resulted in her adopting their attitude toward me. She has no respect for me.

We have five lovely children, and I do not wish to break up the family. However, there is a limit as to how much abuse a person can endure. I have great difficulty in looking forward toward a life of constantly being belittled. I wish my in-laws a long life, but I think that when they are gone, my wife's attitude will not change. What do you suggest?

 All Jews, all over the world, will be bearing scars from the horrors of the Holocaust until the end of time.

There are support groups for "Children of Survivors," and I would suggest you attend these, because you are married to a child of survivors. Perhaps there are now even support groups for *families* of children of survivors. In either case, I believe you can get a better understanding of what is transpiring so that you can make a better adjustment.

It is never pleasant to be insulted and belittled, but there is some truth in the statement that "The only one who can make me feel worthless is I, myself."

The Midrash states that when King Solomon was banished from his throne by the demon Ashmidai, who then took his form and acted as king, Solomon traveled the countryside as a beggar. His insistence, "I am Solomon" was dismissed as the babbling of a lunatic. In describing his state, the Midrash says that at one time he was king over an enormous empire, and at the end he was king only over his walking cane.

Rabbi Chaim Shmulevitz explains this Midrash to mean that Solomon never lost his royal bearings. He was king when heads of nations prostrated themselves before him, and he was also king when he was a beggar and the children of the streets pelted him with stones. Regardless of what anyone else thought of him, he knew who he was.

At the beginning of this book, I quoted the statement of the Rabbi of Kotzk, "If I am I because I am I" etc. The Midrash about Solomon is an excellent example of this. Solomon was king when he ruled over an empire, and to himself he was king when he ruled over only his walking cane. He did not need others to give him an identity. Clearly, Solomon was miserable during these years of exile, but his suffering did not detract from his feeling of self-worth.

It is not impossible that your wife can come around to appreciate you, but this can happen only if you do not crumble under the pressure. By no means would I encourage *gahvah* (vanity), but the irrational idea that you are of less worth because you did not experience the Holocaust yourself is absurd, and should not impact upon you. You must remain strong. Continue in your Torah *shiurim* (classes), and participate in teaching your children Torah.

Facing such an onslaught of degradation from your in-laws, you might profit by some supportive type of therapy. Perhaps you may be able to convince your wife to join you in these sessions, where she may be helped to see the distortions and the unjust nature of her attitude.

You must retain an attitude of respect for your in-laws, since this is required by *halachah*. You should also be able to feel some sympathy for them in spite of how much they have hurt you. Never before in history has there been anything like the Holocaust, and one cannot hold a grudge against anyone who was in that hell.

If at all possible, the marriage should be maintained. There are five children whose only chance at avoiding the ongoing effects of the Holocaust may be their relationship with you.

Correspondence 19

... I attended your lecture where you spoke about the various problems that today appear to be more prevalent among observant people than in the past.

I wonder if this is not due to the rather poor role definition that has occurred in recent times. I am a teacher in a yeshivah, and during the four years I spent in *kollel* we were supported by our parents who supplemented the *kollel* stipend. My wife did not work, and I believe that the Jewish family was built around the traditional role of the husband as provider and the wife as mother and housewife. Today, I see a role reversal in many couples, even among *kollel* couples where wives work to support the husbands' learning. I wonder whether this role reversal and the attitude it represents has not introduced an element of confusion in the family structure . . .

There are indeed many problems today that reflect a deterioration of the wholesomeness of Jewish family life, but it is too simplistic to attribute them to a single factor. Rather than focus on your specific question, I wish to address it in a larger context.

The Jewish family cannot be insulated from the impact of social changes, yet the latter need not have resulted in some of the unfortunate consequences to which we are witness. I happen to believe that a true Torah attitude would have provided greater protection to the family unit. The problem is that for Torah to be effective it must be practiced in its entirety. A precise timepiece will lose its function if even only one tiny part of the mechanism is missing or defective, and the same holds true for Torah.

Accepting Torah as Divinely given at Sinai and the Talmud as the authoritative and hence Divinely inspired interpretation of the Torah, I do not question the validity or seek to have a personally satisfying explanation of any aspect of the Written or Oral Law, and I firmly believe that if this were properly adhered to, the system would function well.

In recent times, western civilization has experienced a major change in the role of the woman. This has caused a significant social upheaval, which has as of yet not subsided. Some women believe that unless women compete with men as full equals in every respect, they are relegating themselves to a traditionally inferior status. The banner of equality represents the loftiest of all human values. Some women who prefer to be housewives and mothers may feel that they are "deserters" who have betrayed their sisters, while some who have gone into the professions or commerce in order to champion this cause, may feel that they are frustrating their prevailing domestic desires. Still others have tried to do both, resulting in an overwhelming demand on their physical and emotional resources.

Those who worship at the shrine of egalitarianism, taking "all people to have been created equal" literally, are simply mistaken. Perhaps they have never heard Pavarotti sing or have never looked at a Rembrandt painting. How foolish it is to assume that all humans are equal. Why does G-d endow one person with greater talent or intellect than another? That is a question to which we have no answer, but the facts speak for themselves.

Nor is it for me to understand why G-d designated some Jews as *Kohanim* (priests) and others as Levites, and gave them special privileges as well as special duties. I do not consider these differences as discriminating, and I do not feel inferior to a *Kohen* or *Levi*.

That halachah assigns different roles to men and women is indisputable. To conclude that these distinctions indicate differences in values is one's personal opinion and is not halachah.

I do not intend to write an apology for halachah. Anyone adequately familiar with the Talmud should know that a woman's modesty and her traditional role as a wife and mother did not detract one iota from her greatness. The matriarch Sarah was superior in prophecy to the patriarch Abraham (*Shemos Rabbah* 1:1) and the greatest of the Talmudic authors, Rabbi Akiva, spoke for all of the wives of Torah scholars when he said to his disciples that all of his Torah scholarship and all of theirs should be attributed to his wife, Rachel. There is a fascinating *Midrash* that describes the pleas of the fathers of the nation following the fall of Jerusalem. The pleas of Abraham, Isaac, Jacob, and Moses, were largely disregarded, and it was only those of the matriarch Rachel that elicited the Divine promise, "It is by virtue of your merit, Rachel, that Israel will be returned to its Land" (*Eichah Rabbah,* Introduction). The Talmud states that Rabbi Yosef, when he heard the footsteps of his mother approaching, would arise and say, "I must stand up before the Divine Presence which is about to enter."

For the wife to work while the husband learns Torah is not a new phenomenon. The Chafetz Chaim's wife was only one among many who ran the store while the husband was in the *beis medrash*.

The issue was not whether the woman should be at home or earning. The woman has the prerogative of doing either, and regardless of where a woman, or for that matter a man, chooses to be, the halachic requirements of *tznius* (modesty) must be observed. These are as applicable to men as they are to women.

A far more serious consideration is that of attitude. Given the proper Torah atmosphere in the home, either or both parents can be working and the family life can be wholesome. In the absence of such an atmosphere, the family can be fragile even with the mother remaining at home. There are any number of families known to me where the traditional roles of father-provider and mother-housewife are intact, yet the family is essentially fragmented.

The requisite Torah atmosphere can be briefly summarized as *kabbalas ol malchus Shomayim* — acceptance of the yoke of Divine sovereignty. This attitude, which one is required to assume daily in reciting the *Shema*, comprises a much broader scope than eating kosher, observing Shabbos, and using the *mikveh*. The term "yoke" in this fundamental principle was intentionally used to convey a total surrender to the will of G-d. Just as the ox functioning under the yoke of the plow has no goal of his own, and works only to fulfill the will of his owner, so must a Torah-observant Jew accept the yoke of Torah as superseding all conceivable goals. This is further elaborated in *Ethics of the Fathers* (2:4), "Set aside your will before His."

There are many observant people who pursue personal goals in life; i.e., their personal economic success, their personal pride, their personal power over others, etc. They may do so completely within the confines of halachah, and yet may be self-serving to a significant degree, rather than totally in the service of G-d. Wherever personal goals assert themselves, there is room for disunity and dissension. The husband may have his goal, the wife hers, and each child his/her own. Where the prevailing attitude is not "What do I want out of life?" but "What does G-d want out of me?" there can be a unity of purpose that can bind the family together. It does not escape me that each person may have one's own version of what G-d wants, and these may indeed be conflicting. Yet, if they are sought sincerely and honestly without selfish considerations, even the differences need not disrupt family unity.

It is easy to speak about total surrender of one's will to that of G-d, but it is quite difficult to implement. Our individual cravings are powerful influences in determining our behavior. The point that I am making is where surrender of personal will occurs, as I am certain prevailed in the lives of the great *tzaddikim,* the family unity and the development of the children was not negatively affected by the wife being in charge of the business. Neither role maintenance nor role reversal was significant.

Unfortunately, such total surrender is not found even among very observant families. Secular values have crept in, however subtly, and have affected the wholesomeness of many contemporary observant families.

I have seen many situations where the wife has worked to put the husband through professional school, e.g., medicine or law. In a number of these cases the result was unfortunate, in that the successful doctor or lawyer later lost interest in his spouse, and the marriage was terminated. Very often the problem was one of ego, in that the husband felt himself to be beholden to his wife for having sacrificed so much to enable him to achieve a career. Like many people who have difficulty in accepting from a benefactor and bear resentments towards their benefactor, in this case perhaps coupled with a feeling of guilt for having "exploited" her, he subsequently turned against her.

I believe that the Chafetz Chaim, who dedicated himself totally to Torah study while his wife ran their store, did not feel he was exploiting her or that she was sacrificing for him. I believe they both shared a *kabbalas ol malchus Shomayim,* in that both were doing that which they were convinced G-d wished them to do.

"Kabbalas ol" may seem like a tall order, but I assure you, it is not my own invention. Perhaps not too many people attain it in its full sense, but that does not deter it from its validity. People often have questions about certain aspects of halachah, which to their way of thinking, are not quite equitable. Often this means that they are not in keeping with the concepts of right and wrong that prevail in western civilization. The argument by some women that halachah

favors men over women is one such example. The answer to these questions is found in *Psalms* (19:10): "The laws of G-d are true; they are just when taken together." Any single halachah may impress someone as being less than fair, but when Torah is taken in its totality, then the justness of all its commandments is evident. *Kabbalas ol* is part of the integral package.

There are some aspects in halachah which are not routinely observed, and a wrong impression may therefore result. For example, it is common practice that when a respected Torah scholar enters the room, everyone rises. Yet, if the wife of the scholar were to enter the room, her presence might not be acknowledged in the same way. This is in violation of the Talmud which states that the wife of a scholar commands the same reverence as the scholar (*Shavuos* 30b), a halachah which follows the comment of Rabbi Akiva quoted earlier.

For various reasons, some quite legitimate, the secular world has raised the issue of the inferior role of woman in society, and has tried to rectify this by various egalitarian maneuvers, many of which have failed. For example, the successful male executive feels fulfilled in his professional achievement, whereas the successful female executive who also has the duties of a wife and mother, may feel that she is depriving her family of her presence in the home, hence she does not feel fulfilled even with a successful career. If she has foregone a family in favor of a career, she may feel herself lacking in that dimension. Western civilization has created an unsolvable dilemma for the modern woman. But then, the secular world does not have a concept of "*Kabbalas ol*" which supersedes all else. The contemporary woman, who is part of a family that operates under true *kabbalas ol,* can have a healthy self-esteem whether she is in the home full time, works outside the home, or has a professional career. Since self-esteem has a ripple effect, children raised in such a home are likely to develop self-esteem and self-confidence, and to benefit from the strength of the family union.

To summarize, we find ourselves in difficulty because we believe we are living Torah-true lives, yet we do not seem to be reaping the promised benefits thereof. What has happened, however, is that although we may be complying with halachah, many of us are missing the essence of Torah-true living, and are particularly vulnerable to the many impacts of the secular world in which we live. While the latter may not have impinged on our ritual practices, it may have affected our value system to a far greater degree than we suspect.

Today's observant Jew cannot therefore be content with being *Shulchan Aruch*-compliant. He must be a thorough *Mesilas Yesharim* (*Path of the Just*) person, practicing the principles of *mussar* and *chassidus* in one's daily life with no less dedication than one observes Shabbos and *kashrus*.

Correspondence 20

. . . At age twenty-one, I married and spent two years in *kollel*. I then entered into my father-in-law's business. Whereas we had previously had a very pleasant relationship, I now discovered an entirely different person. In the business he was an absolute tyrant, shouting at everyone if things were not done exactly his way (even if it was wrong). His employees despised him, but humored him in order to retain their jobs. I could never satisfy him, and he constantly put me down. Before long this attitude carried over to our home life, and he derided me in front of my wife.

I had no choice but to leave and to go into business for myself. Unfortunately my venture did not succeed, and this proved to him that I was a *shlemazel,* and he began urging my wife to get a divorce. He is a very domineering person, and forced divorce upon us. We have one child.

I am now three years post-divorce and am not able to get hold of myself. I work as a salesman but I feel totally crushed. I see my child every two weeks, and I don't know what my wife's true feelings are. Maybe if I proved myself successful in business, he would gain respect for me and allow us to reconcile.

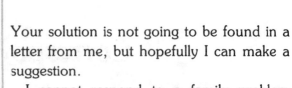Your solution is not going to be found in a letter from me, but hopefully I can make a suggestion.

I cannot respond to a family problem without having much more information about what happened. I have your version, but I do not have your wife's. Things may indeed be essentially as you describe them, but there may be other factors that she might add which are important.

Let me address one point that you made. While it is never pleasant to be derided, or even worse, to be cut to ribbons by a tyrannical person, there is a psychological principle that no one can make me feel worthless except myself. If I were to insult you and call you offensive names; e.g., thief, murderer, etc., you would certainly be displeased, but you would see this as my problem in that I have a propensity towards making unwarranted accusations. Knowing that you are none of these things, my nasty comments would not penetrate. It is totally different when a person consciously or subconsciously believes that the things said about him are or may be true, in which case the remarks penetrate down to the bone.

Many people have a low self-esteem, feeling themselves unworthy or incompetent without any basis in fact for these feelings. They are most vulnerable to be deeply affected by comments that they are inadequate, because they indeed believe this to be true. Obviously, the solution to this is to develop a healthy self-esteem.

While I know little about your father-in-law other than what you describe, I am familiar with personalities of this type. There are some people who are born with a talent for business, and can not only sell ice to Eskimos, but if dropped in the midst of the desert, would find a way to sell thorns to cactuses. The only thing they really value is money. Why, then, would such a person choose a *yeshivah bochur* as a husband for his daughter? After all, yeshivah education is not exactly conducive to the development of financial wizardry. He does so because it is an ego thing for him, and this is what his friends are doing. As long as the young man remains in *kollel,* he values him for his own ego. If the young man becomes a rabbi or goes into *chinuch,* it can still satisfy his ego. But if he should venture into the business world, which is the father-in-law's area of expertise, and not perform up to the latter's standards, the result may be disastrous. He may have little true respect for Torah, and thus when his ego is not satisfied and the young man does not excel in business, he loses all respect for him.

You should realize that your true value is as a *ben Torah,* and to the extent that you fulfill yourself in Torah while earning a livelihood, you should not feel inadequate. Whether the dissolution of your marriage is due to your wife's sharing your father-in-law's values or being dominated by him, you should not see this as a failure on your part, although the pain of the loss of the marriage is not minimized by this.

As I mentioned, you may well have had some self-esteem problems that antedated your marriage, and these should be corrected. There are some fine therapists in your community, and several names are appended to this letter.

Again, I have no access to other information about yourself other than what you have provided. In therapy you will be able to provide additional data that should help resolve your problems and give you the courage and strength to rebuild your life and be successful.

Correspondence 21

(Rather than a correspondence, this segment was the result of a personal interview. The questioner is unable to write. The interview is not presented verbatim, but does convey the idea of the questioner.)

... I am now 22, and for the past two years I have been a student at a *baal teshuvah* yeshivah.

I was a slow student as a child, and although it was known that I had a learning disability, the exact nature of it was not determined. I was given extra help with tutors, and passed along from class to class. I never learned how to write more than a few simple sentences, and my reading is fragmentary. My parents were always very loving and caring, and their attitude was a very protective one; "Don't push Moshe too much. He can't handle it." I can truly say that they did not love me any less because of my limitations, but it was a love mixed with pity. They loved me in a different way than they loved my "normal" brother. I received the same kind of consideration from my teachers, who were thoughtful enough not to call on me in order to avoid embarrassing me in front of the class.

Needless to say, I grew up with enormous shame. Call it what you might, I was not equal to my siblings and peers. I remember trying to gain acceptance by giving candy to my friends, and trying to be as helpful as I could to people. I was desperate to get people to accept me and like me even though I was "the dumb kid."

I left school at sixteen and took a job. I was always the first at work in the morning and the last to leave at night. I wanted the boss to like me. I learned my task very well, and I did come to realize that I had skills. I have an excellent memory, which I need because I can't write.

When I came to the yeshiva and tried to learn Hebrew, it was suspected that I was dyslexic. They told me it had nothing to do with intelligence, and that I could still be helped with it, although had it been taken care of when I was a child, the results would have been far better.

My problem is that I am just one big chunk of shame. Sometimes I think that I would like to do something with my skills. I think I could succeed in business. But most of the time I just prefer to remain where I am. Doing anything different will be hard. I am already accustomed to being the "dumb kid" who does things for everybody, and as a rule I am comfortable doing that. Any change would cause discomfort, and I don't know why I should rock the boat. . .

It is particularly tragic when preventable problems occur. Children with learning disabilities or hearing difficulties are sometimes labeled as slow learners or mentally retarded, and the harm that results from this oversight, as in your case, is far reaching.

One of the points your case makes is the fallacy of the theory that if one understands the cause of a problem, that alleviates it. You clearly understand that you are intelligent and have some fine talents, and that your having considered yourself to be "the dumb kid" was due to a learning disability which is no reflection whatever on your intelligence. Yet, although you recognize that the source of your feeling inferior was a distortion, the feeling has not disappeared, and the pattern of psychological defenses, especially "people pleasing" has continued.

Children who are indeed incapable of grasping things very often develop an attitude of defeatism. "What's the use of trying? I can't get it anyway." Not infrequently, however, children who are perfectly capable of grasping, say, mathematical principles and problems, may nevertheless turn off and develop a mental block, whereby they refuse to try. They then fall behind in math, and unless this is picked up by an astute teacher, they may fall so far behind that only an aggressive motivational program can bring them out of their rut.

You seem to have developed this defeatist attitude, so that instead of exercising the potential you have, you prefer to remain in a rut because getting out "may cause discomfort."

The saving grace is that you came to consult someone about this. In other words, your decision to stay in the rut is not final, else you would not be asking what to do. You obviously, therefore, are not only aware that you can perform, but also are not ready to totally surrender. What you need is a good push in the right direction.

Merely telling you what to do is not enough. You are going to have to work at it and put forth a great deal of energy. The natural inertia within you may cause you to give up when you must exert yourself to overcome obstacles, and you are going to need a constant source of motivation.

Furthermore, established habit patterns are often difficult to change. Your tendency to ingratiate yourself by various "people pleasing" maneuvers is likely to persist in spite of your awareness of what and why you are doing it. If you try to straighten a bent branch, it will promptly revert to its former position, and in order to straighten it you must compensate in the opposite direction and continue to hold the branch in that position for an extended period of time. Similarly, even if you start changing the defensive maneuvers that resulted from your self-image distortion, they are likely to recur.

You therefore need the proper therapy and guidance to overcome your reluctance to assert yourself and your "people pleasing" behavior. This will require both time and effort to reverse a behavior pattern of long standing. I strongly urge that you avail yourself of treatment by a "cognitive therapist." This school is most adept at bringing about the necessary corrections.

Unless you do so now, the behavior pattern will not only persist, but will reinforce itself and intensify. In ten years you will be 32, and if you do not correct the problem now, you will look back with deep regret. Today you may think that remaining in the rut and taking the path of least resistance is the most comfortable thing to do. I assure you that later in life it will prove terribly uncomfortable, but by the time you come to feel that the disadvantages of inaction outweigh the comfort of inertia, the difficulty of making the necessary changes will be infinitely greater than it is at present.

There is a Midrash that states that the word "now" refers to *teshuva* (*Bereishis Rabba* 21:6). Just as delay in changing sinful behavior allows the latter to become more entrenched and more resistive to change, so does delay in making any personality change allow for progression and reinforcement of undesirable traits. Pick up the phone and make your appointment now, today!

Correspondence 22

 . . . When I read your book, *Let Us Make Man*, it was like a new world opened up before me. I had never realized that I was operating under a completely false self-conception. I did not go into therapy, but was able to look at myself more clearly. I had been depressed ever since I can remember, and at age twenty-six was able to effect a complete reversal in the way I felt about myself. My marriage improved, my work performance increased so dramatically that I won a prize as the firm's best salesman. I meant to write to express my gratitude for your help, but somehow I never got around to it.

I am writing to you now because I have suffered a relapse. About four months ago, the firm where I was employed abruptly went out of business. As of now, I have not found another job. My wife is very supportive and encouraging, but I feel the old gloom and the sense of failure and depression all over again. The four good years seem to be nothing but a pleasant dream from which I have awoken into the stark reality of my inabilities and limitations . . .

First of all, I am pleased that you were able to dispose of the negative self-image and see the real self. Secondly, the relapse you describe is a quite common phenomenon.

Let me suggest a simple experiment. Take a piece of thick cardboard, and fold over one corner. Now straighten out the corner. You will note that even if you were to press the crease with a flat iron, the mark where it had been folded will not disappear. If you exert a slight pressure at any other point of the cardboard to bend it, you will encounter some resistance, because the cardboard is stiff and will not yield easily. However, at the area where it had once been folded, even a very slight pressure will cause it to bend, because the persistent mark is one of low resistance.

A person may recover from poor self-esteem and function to one's new self-awareness, but one is very vulnerable to the resurgence of the low self-esteem, sometimes even in reaction to minor pressures. The loss of a job is certainly not a minor pressure, because the feeling of providing for one's family is a major ego component. It is not at all surprising that this experience resulted in a reactivation of the low self-esteem, similar to bending the cardboard at the mark of the previous fold.

To be on the alert is to be prepared. There are numerous incidents in life that can trigger a relapse, and when this occurs, one should not be devastated. Indeed, learning how to respond after suffering a self-esteem relapse may be the best preparation for avoiding another. It is a mistake to think that a relapse takes a person back to square one. The progress you have made is never lost.

Let me tell you about a little incident that may shed some light on the subject. One winter day I had to mail a registered letter at the post office, and since my car refused to start, I walked the snow-covered six blocks, being careful to avoid icy patches. In spite of my caution, I slipped and hurt myself, but fortunately was not harmed. Clearly, lying on the sidewalk and feeling sorry for myself would have gotten me nowhere. I rose and made my way to my destination, walking even more carefully for the rest of the way.

Two things were very evident. (1) The progress of the three blocks I had made prior to the fall was not lost. I had advanced towards my goal. (2) I was now more cautious, and more aware of where the slippery spots might be, and perhaps this greater caution prevented a more serious fall later, which might have otherwise occurred and have been truly harmful.

The *Tanya* points out that progress in one's spiritual life is characterized by temporary reversals, which are intervals between growth spurts, and explains the verse in *Proverbs* (24:16), "A righteous person may fall seven times and arise," as referring to this phenomenon. It is of interest that there is also a similar concept in psychology of "regression in the service of the ego."

When such regressions occur, they may be subjectively experienced as devastating, yet after the reversal the person may be at a much higher spiritual level than he had been in the past, and must now regroup his energies for the next upward climb.

This pattern is as true of progress in self-esteem as it is of spirituality. Your progress in self-esteem was not erased by your relapse, and you now know that since these regressions are part of the course, you must brace yourself for further growth challenges.

Although you appeared to have done well without professional help, you might consider the extra advantage of a more thorough self-awareness with the help of a therapist, and I will gladly provide you with some referrals in your area.

Correspondence 23

. . . I am twenty-seven, single, and have just received a master's degree in engineering. Several years ago, I spent six months in Israel, and was introduced to a *baal teshuvah* yeshivah, where I discovered I was totally ignorant of anything Jewish. I began learning to read Hebrew and some *Chumash*. On my return, I continued to learn in a local yeshivah while going to college.

I am now at a loss what to do with myself. Part of me says to take two years and study intensively in a yeshivah. On the other hand, my job opportunities are best now. If I apply for a job with a two year hiatus after graduation, not only will I have become a bit rusty, but many employers will not understand why I wasn't employed for two years, and telling them that I was in a yeshivah is not likely to quell their suspicions.

I am very desirous of living in Israel. I am uncertain whether to start work here and at least begin to save up some money to be able to get a better start in Israel, or whether to move now. I think that with my degree, I could probably get a job there.

I must also admit that my being a *baal teshuvah* has caused me much confusion. I get the feeling that the people who worked with me are somewhat like the fighter pilots in the war, who would make a mark on their planes for each enemy aircraft they shot down. Sometimes I think there is a race to see who can convert more people to *teshuvah*. Also, while I see the beauty of Torah, I am distressed by the behavior of some of the religious community, whose religious observance does not seem to have deterred them from corrupt and even immoral behavior.

While I do learn as much as I can, I feel I need a guide to lead me through this haze. I want to do the right thing and not mess up the one life I have.

I was very influenced by your books, *Living Each Day* and *Generation to Generation*. I might be able to find a job in Pittsburgh and avail myself of your guidance.

 I am deeply moved by your flattering comments, and while I do not feign humility, I must tell you that the books you refer to do not qualify me as an authority to resolve your problem. *Living Each Day* is an anthology, a compilation of various excerpts from Torah literature arranged in convenient, daily, bite-sized portions. *Generation to Generation* is a recollection of stories and memories. There is not a single word of originality in either, so that these books do not attest to any particular innovative skills on my part.

As a practicing psychiatrist I have worked with people who have had various emotional problems, and while I have developed some expertise in this, it again does not qualify me as an adviser to someone who does not have an emotional or mental problem, but is rather in need of some reality guidance. I am not sure that a psychiatrist is really that much more qualified to provide this than a surgeon or a dentist. My expertise is in working with illness, not with healthy issues.

There may indeed be some people, particularly Torah scholars, who have familiarized themselves with adjustment problems, and can serve as counselors. There is also value in talking with a psychotherapist, not necessarily because you need treatment, but to have a listening ear which is attached to a person who can be objective and help you clarify for yourself what your most advisable course is. In either case, the ultimate decision must be yours. It would be pleasant to be able to be told by someone what to do, and to be relieved of the responsibility of decision making, but unfortunately there are no such oracles. You do the best you can, and pray to G-d to guide you in the correct path.

I can only mention some ideas that come to mind. I certainly sympathize with someone who discovers in adult life that one was unfairly deprived of a Jewish education, and that there is so much to learn in Torah. In some circumstances, it may be advisable to take time off for intensive study, but the drawbacks you have cited cannot be easily dismissed. However, it is certainly possible to continue one's Torah education even while working. One must learn to schedule properly and how to economize one's time. If the time many people spent watching television, reading non-essential material, and engaging in other pastimes were all put to constructive use, a great deal of learning could be achieved daily, let alone on weekends.

I can easily understand your desire to live in Israel, but if it is more practical to start your career here, you still have time to make the move. It becomes much more difficult when one has a family with growing children, but if you can begin to work now and hopefully marry in the near future, you still have time to make the move without much difficulty.

The problem you cite of observant Jews whose behavior is inconsistent with Torah is not a new one. There have always been some people who have chosen which Torah laws they feel apply to them and which they may ignore. These are misguided people, whose appearance as observant Jews has led some people to ridicule Torah observance. Such people's behavior is not a reflection on Torah, but only on themselves. There are many, many people who practice the ethics of Torah as well as the rituals, but these are people who mind their own business and thus their activities and behavior are not discussed in the sensationalism of the media, hence no one pays much attention to their existence. A person who wishes to live a true Torah life should avail oneself of the great works of ethics, such as *Path of the Just*, and fashion one's life accordingly.

You may have noted in my writings that I frequently refer to the problem of self-esteem. A healthy self-esteem includes confidence in making decisions for oneself. I believe that every person has the capacity to make proper decisions for himself, but we may not trust ourselves sufficiently in that respect.

The decision-making process may be encumbered by various pressures and drives that may not be in one's best interest, yet a person may not be aware of the influences that bear down on the decision-making process. Elucidating the issues with a counselor or therapist can help identify these and allow you to implement your decision-making skills, which I am sure you have.

I cannot encourage you to come to Pittsburgh. I am now spending major segments of time in Israel, and even when in the United States, I am often away from Pittsburgh. Furthermore, the particular type of work that I do does not permit scheduling regular sessions. I would recommend that you see someone in your own community, who can give you the time you need to work things out, and I will be glad to recommend several competent people to you.

Correspondence 24

. . . I have a problem regarding my marriage and I don't know to whom I can turn.

I am now 27, and have been married four years. We have two children.

My wife comes from a fine Torah family, and her parents are fond of me. When we were going out, I found her attractive, we had the same *hashkofos* (perspectives) and goals, and I saw no reason not to marry her.

Was I madly in love? Probably not, although I have nothing to gauge my feelings by.

At any rate, about two years into the marriage I realized it was really a kind of neutral relationship. She is a very fine person, devoted to me and the children, everything one could ask for, but I just don't feel much love for her, if any. I can't tell you why I feel this way, but just that I do.

I've been postponing taking action, hoping my feelings would change, but they haven't. I look at other couples in our circle and they seem to be much happier. For example, if she leaves to visit her parents for a few days, I don't miss her. In case you might think I have been attracted to someone else, that is not the case.

I don't know what to do about this. I don't want to hurt her, because she has done nothing to deserve being hurt. Yet I cannot see myself living for the rest of my life in a loveless marriage. . .

While it is risky to jump to conclusions without a personal and detailed interview, I am going to give you an opinion. Of course, this should be taken only as an educated guess, and I strongly urge that you do have a thorough consultation with a psychologist.

When all of the ingredients for a successful relationship exist, yet the emotions are not there, one must look at why one is not feeling what one should be feeling. It is, of course, possible that although two people seem to be perfectly compatible on the basis of all known factors, there may be that the poorly-defined, intangible "chemistry" that is missing, and this chemistry is either there or not there. It cannot be created. In such a case, we might well assume that this nebulous ingredient might be present in a relationship with another person. On the basis of my experience with similar cases, of which there have been a number, I suspect that it is not a question of chemistry, but of something within yourself that requires attention.

Let me first mention a common misconception. I don't know how much exposure you have had to the media, but what is so often portrayed in the media as "love" is little more than animal passion. Anyone foolish enough to fantasize that this is the fabric of which a stable marriage is made is certain to be deeply disappointed. This may be a major contributing factor to the extraordinary high divorce rate in western civilization.

The observation that others appear to be happier than you is one of the pitfalls of judging your "insides" by other people's "outsides." You see only what others want you to see, and I am certain that others who have observed you have probably thought that you have a blissful marriage. As a rule, no one displays their dissatisfaction publicly.

There is at least an implication that you are considering leaving a "loveless" marriage. This might be a tragic mistake. The loneliness that would follow may be devastating, and I suspect that if and when you enter a new relationship, it might not be any more satisfying than this one. If one is dissatisfied with the programming, buying a new radio does not help at all.

I suspect that your problem in not feeling love has little to do with your wife, and much more to do with you. Many people are incapable of feeling love. They may *think* that they feel love, while in fact they feel only a physical passion, which is usually of brief duration.

While there are various barriers to feeling love, one of the most common is that one can love another only when one feels deserving of being loved oneself. This is contained in Solomon's statement, "Like the reflection in the water, so is the heart of one person to another" (Proverbs 27:19). Love is not a one-way affair. One cannot be loved unless one loves, and one cannot love unless one is loved. The person who feels incapable of being loved cannot love another.

As with many other emotional problems, the culprit is likely to be a low self-esteem, a feeling of unworthiness that haunts many people from childhood on throughout life. Children who feel undeserving of being loved often take on duties in the home or do other things to ingratiate themselves, in the hope of earning love. This pattern may be sustained throughout life. Others may draw attention to themselves in the hopes of achieving recognition, which they may confuse with love. There is nothing that can undermine a marriage as much as a feeling of unworthiness, of not deserving to be loved.

People who feel themselves undeserving of love may sometimes develop a relationship based on their being helpful to a person, as when a doctor or nurse marries someone whom he/she treated or helped care for. The unspoken statement in such a relationship is, "I may not deserve your love for what I am, but I do deserve it for what I did for you." Sometimes a relationship like this may end up with an "allegiance" to the rescuer, rather than love.

A person may sometimes marry someone far beneath him/her socially, intellectually, or who is considered inferior in any other way. The unspoken statement here is, "Of course you will love me.

Perhaps I do not merit being loved by a peer, but given the disparity between us, you should certainly appreciate me." In this case, admiration and gratitude may masquerade as love. I have cited just a few examples, but the variations are kaleidoscopic.

There is a widespread tendency for people who are dissatisfied to make a change of some sort in the hope that this change will eliminate their problem. They may change jobs, places of residence, or even spouses. The one important change they should really be making, namely changing oneself, is not accomplished too frequently.

In *Generation to Generation* (CIS, 1987), I tell a story that I used to hear very frequently from my mother as a bedtime story, but whose message did not impact upon me until some forty years later.

A peasant who made his living by hewing stones out of a mountain, frequently would bewail his fate, railing against the injustice that some people are born into wealth, whereas he must do back-breaking work from dawn to dusk to provide mere subsistence for his family. One day, as he was swinging his heavy pick-axe, he heard a tumultuous noise from afar. Climbing to the top of the mountain, he could see in the distance a royal parade in progress. The king was riding in a coach drawn by six white horses, and on both sides of the road throngs were shouting "Bravo!", and throwing flowers at the royal coach.

The stonecutter raised his eyes to Heaven. "Dear G-d," he said, "why should there be such a disparity between people? I am a human being just like the king, but he is mighty and all-powerful, and I am a nothing. Since You are a just G-d, You should grant me that I could be mighty and powerful, and that I could be the king."

This happened to be a propitious moment, and the peasant suddenly found himself transformed into the king, riding in the parade and receiving the accolades of thousands. He basked in the glory of being mighty and powerful. But then he began to feel very uncomfortable. The sun was beating down on him mercilessly, and since he was dressed in his heavy royal robes, he just wilted away.

"How strange!" he said. "I thought I was the mightiest force in the world. Clearly the sun is much mightier than I am. I therefore wish to be the sun."

He was then turned into the sun, and thoroughly enjoyed being the most powerful force in the world. However, he began to feel frustrated, because a dark cloud had moved beneath him, and formed a barrier to his light. "Aha! If a cloud can defy the sun, then it must be more powerful than the sun. I wish to be that cloud." He then enjoyed his power at being able to frustrate the sun.

Suddenly he felt himself swept away by a powerful gust of wind. "What is this?" he said. "If the wind can drive a cloud any way it wishes, it must be more powerful than the cloud. I now wish to be the wind." Once he was transformed into the wind, he frolicked about doing much mischief, whipping up hurricanes, and devastating entire forests. "I am truly the mightiest," he said.

But then he found himself stymied. He had run headlong into a tall mountain which we could not budge. "Aha!" he said. "The mountain can withstand the force of the wind, so it is even more powerful. I wish to be that mountain." He then stood majestically with his snowcapped peak reaching into the sky, ruling, as it were, over the entire country.

This reign was disturbed by a sharp pain. A stonecutter wielding a pick-axe was tearing pieces out of him. "So!" he said. "If a stone cutter can dismantle a mountain, then he must be even more powerful. I wish to be that stonecutter." He then became the most powerful of all: a stonecutter.

When I heard this story at age five, I had no idea what it meant, other than being a charming bedtime story. Many, many years later, when people with emotional problems consulted me and suggested making changes in their occupation or marriage, I only then realized what my mother had taught me. If a person is satisfied with oneself, it is quite easy to be content with anything. If one is not satisfied with oneself, situational changes are not likely to provide more than momentary relief.

I would suggest you avail yourself of a psychologic evaluation, which may well reveal the basis for your inability to feel love for another, which I strongly suspect may be due to your inability to feel that you *can be loved*. Resolving the problem will make you happier and more effective as an individual as well as a husband and father.

Correspondence 25

. . .We have a problem which is nothing less than a calamity, and we are at wits end what to do.

We are a *frum* family. My father is nearing retirement. I do not live near my parents, which is why I did not know what was happening.

My younger brother, 34, is married and has six children. He had a job, and we assumed he was working. I now find out that several years ago he began asking my father for sums of money under various pretexts, and my father naively believed him. My father is not a rich man by any means, but managed to gather the money. My brother is very clever and could sell ice to the Eskimos, and my father trusted him.

Last year my father received calls from two friends apprising him of the fact my brother had borrowed money from them and had not repaid it. My father paid them, and my brother gave him some explanations, which he again believed.

In the past few weeks the truth has emerged. My brother is a gambler and is deeply in debt. He has taken out a home equity loan, and has emptied the children's bank accounts. He has not been at his job for months. When I heard about this I flew home. His wife knows nothing about this and he begged us not to tell her. He promises he will never gamble again. He owes many thousands of dollars, and is asking us to pay off his debts, stating that he owes some money to the mob who may kill him if he does not pay. We do not have that kind of money, and all the members of the family put together would have to go into debt. Oh, yes. I now found out that he had written bad checks which my father covered, and also had borrowed on someone else's credit cards, which my father paid off to avoid a *chilul Hashem* (scandal). We are desperate. Please help!

The story you relate is new to you, but is a very common description of a compulsive or addictive gambler. There are striking similarities between compulsive gambling and addictions, such as alcohol or drugs. Let me first tell you what *not* to do.

An addict, whether alcoholic or gambler, will not change without treatment, and is not likely to accept treatment unless he is absolutely forced to. This coercion to treatment and to change his lifestyle can come only if he feels the misery which his gambling has caused. If anyone does *anything* that will relieve this misery, this is contributing to prolongation of the gambling. Your father acted like most other parents, with good intentions, which only helped sustain the problem.

Your brother's promises are absolutely worthless. He may cry and swear on a stack of Bibles that he will never gamble again, and he may even be sincere in his pledges, but he will not keep them because the intensity of the compulsion in compulsive gambling will override any promises. The only hope is appropriate treatment.

It would be the worst possible mistake if the family were to try to pay off his debts. If you try to avoid the *chilul Hashem* of his bad check writing and other dishonest acts, you will only have to face the same problem a bit later when he will owe amounts that are beyond everyone's most extreme means. As unpleasant as it is, the ultimate exposure cannot be avoided, and it is foolish to consider this as a deterrent to the necessary action.

Addictive conditions, whether alcoholism or compulsive gambling, are very similar to cancer. They do not go away by themselves, and if unattended, invariably get worse and kill. As with cancer, the treatment may require drastic measures, and are not without risk. These are:

1. No more bailouts of any kind.

2. Your brother's wife must be apprised of everything. It is unconscionable to keep her in the dark. She is a person with rights, and must consider her own future and that of her children. She may be shocked to find that he has already sold some or all of her valuable jewelry which she assumed had been lost or stolen. Furthermore, her participation in his recovery is absolutely essential.

3. Everyone in the family must learn all they can about compulsive gambling. There are groups of family members of compulsive gamblers who have meetings to learn more about the problem, how to live with it, what to do, and what not to do. These groups are known as Gam-Anon, and can be reached by calling Gamblers Anonymous, which is listed in the telephone directory.

4. Getting your brother into treatment. I list this step after the first three, because unless those are undertaken first, he is unlikely to accept treatment. His attending Gamblers Anonymous meetings is crucial, but it is very helpful to first begin with an intensive treatment program. There are several of these available and I am appending their names and phone numbers to this letter.

What about his threat that the mob will get him if his debts are not paid? In Gam-Anon the family will learn how to deal with such threats, and in treatment and GA he will also learn how to handle these. He is not the first gambler to encounter this problem.

What if he refuses treatment? This too will be addressed in the Gam-Anon family groups. All the problems your family has had and will have have already occurred to others, and the voice of experience is worth heeding.

Is it possible that if your rescue efforts are stopped he will become desperate and may commit suicide? This cannot be excluded. But even such a dread possibility cannot stop you from taking the necessary action, because otherwise the threat of suicide will be used as blackmail, which is without limits. Everyone's homes, savings, and reputation can be sacrificed in response to a suicide threat, and after all is said and done, the condition remains unchanged.

Is there any hope? Definitely. There are compulsive gamblers who have recovered and live happy lives with their families, but none of these recovered until they had hit "rock bottom" where there was no way to go but up.

The one expense that the family may have to bear is for the intensive treatment program, which is not likely to be inexpensive. But again, no bailouts. If he writes bad checks or does other dishonest things, charges must be pressed and he must feel the full impact of his actions, including imprisonment if that is the case. The family should not post bail nor hire an attorney for him. He must deal with the consequences of his behavior.

I am sorry that I must paint such a bleak picture for you. Although there is hope, it is only when there is proper action on the part of the family that such hope can be realized.

Correspondence 26

I am a *baal teshuvah*, thirty-one, married, and we have three children. My family was non-observant, and we were "Rosh Hashanah-Yom Kippur Jews." When my grandmother moved in with us, we began keeping kosher to accommodate her, but we continued to eat non-kosher food outside the home. I had the usual bar mitzvah training, barely learning how to read Hebrew.

At age fifteen, I met some NCSY students and gradually became more *frum*. My parents were not too happy, but did not object, even when I went to yeshivah at sixteen. I am an accountant, and at twenty-four I married. We decided to make *aliyah,* and I found a job in Israel. We moved into a very *frum* neighborhood.

Shortly after we came here, I began to feel a dark cloud descending over me, and I don't know why. I have three lovely children and a wonderful devoted wife, and am earning a living. I have a daily *shiur*, and I should be happy, but I am not. I think I project my unhappiness over my entire family. My wife says she does not even remember me smiling anymore.

I take my *Yiddishkeit* very seriously. I know I am here to serve Hashem, and that life is a serious business not to be taken lightly.

But others who are equally committed don't seem to be miserable. Sometimes I think I am being punished for all the wrong things I did before I became *frum*.

There is nothing really that can make me laugh. I grew up watching comedy shows on TV, which I no longer possess. I used to enjoy the jokes in the Reader's Digest, but I don't have anything like that here. I talked to a *rav,* and he suggested I learn about *simchah* in some *seforim.* I've tried to do that, but it isn't enough. I don't know if anyone can understand what I'm going through.

 I don't wish to let your letter go unanswered, but I don't know that I am really the right person to reply to your question. There are some problems in adjusting to a radically different lifestyle that cannot be fully understood by someone born into a *frum* home. There are a number of psychologists and rabbis that share your background, and they may be more qualified to address your problem.

One young man who had been *shomer mitzvos* for about eight years gave a somewhat similar description of how he felt, and when I pointed out that *Yiddishkeit* was meant to be enjoyed, he said, "That's easy for you to say. When you walk by a *treifah* restaurant, you are probably oblivious to its very existence. I still must make a conscious decision not to go in. Even after eight years, *treifah* is not the automatic turn-off for me that it is for you."

From a pure energy economy perspective, I can easily understand this. The *baal teshuvah* must use energy for many things that are reflex actions for someone *frum* from birth. Until such responses become automatic, the *baal teshuvah* may have a drain on his energies, and perhaps simply not have enough left over to invest in anything more than remaining observant of Torah. This may change at different times for different people.

Yiddishkeit should indeed be taken seriously, regardless whether one is *frum* from birth or a *baal teshuvah,* but "seriously" does not mean morosely. For example, the Talmud states that one must pray with an attitude of *koved rosh* (utmost seriousness) while at the same time with *simchah shel mitzvah* (the joy of doing a *mitzvah*) (Berachos 30b-31a).

The Baal Shem Tov visited a town where the townspeople complained that their *chazan* (cantor) chanted the *Al Cheit* (prayer of confession) with a lively melody, which they felt was inconsistent with enumerating one's sins and asking for forgiveness. The Baal Shem Tov asked the *chazan* for an explanation, and the latter stated that every person is a sanctuary for the Divine Spirit, and that a sin soils the place where the Spirit of G-d must rest. When one confesses one's sins and does *teshuvah*, one is thereby cleansing oneself. "Should I not rejoice when I am beautifying the sanctuary for the Divine Presence?" The Baal Shem Tov thoroughly agreed. We can thus see that there is a way in which one can deal with *teshuvah*, with sincere regret for having done wrong, while maintaining an attitude of *simchah.*

I do not understand your reference to feeling guilty for the "wrongs" you have done before you became aware of *Yiddishkeit.* It should be obvious that a child raised in a non-observant environment, who adopts parental standards of right and wrong, cannot be held responsible for parental errors. Incidents that happened before you became observant should not induce any guilt feelings whatever.

If you are referring to improprieties that occurred after you became observant, which do require *teshuvah*, there is nevertheless no reason to let these depress you. Indeed, any effective learning generally results from mistakes, and the Talmud states that a person does not get a firm grip on halachah until he has transgressed it (*Gittin* 43a). Realizing that one has erred is a learning experience, and we must be able to see the redeeming features in a growth experience.

The absence of television is not a cause for regret. Other than an occasional documentary, many current television programs are so decadent and degenerate in morals and violence, and this includes the so-called comedy shows, that having a television at home where there are growing, impressionable children whose exposure cannot be limited to cartoons is jeopardizing the development of proper morals. Most of the things that are considered amusing and entertaining on modern television are not only improper for a *ben-Torah,* but for every decent person as well.

However, there should be many things that a family can enjoy and which can allow them to laugh together. I do not feel that *leitzanus* should be translated as humor, but rather as mockery and ridicule. These are forbidden by Torah because they degrade the object at which they are directed. It is not only forbidden to ridicule anything which is sacred, but even ridiculing another person is forbidden. This does not mean that one should not enjoy a funny story that is in good taste.

This is the primary reason why I wrote the book, *Smiling Each Day* (Mesorah, 1993). I wished to demonstrate that there is wit and healthy humor to be found in Torah literature and in some of the anecdotes of our great *tzaddikim.*

It is a great mistake to believe that *Yiddishkeit* requires a constantly serious demeanor. This attitude may lead to *atzvus* (dejection), and the chassidic master of Karlin said that although the Torah does not explicitly state that dejection is forbidden, there is nothing that is as conducive to sin as dejection.

Rabbeinu Bachya, one of the foremost Torah ethicists, states in his *magnum opus, Duties of the Heart,* that the truly pious person is "externally cheerful, while internally broken-hearted." This does not mean that one dissimulates, because Rabbeinu Bachya would never condone a sham, let alone recommend it. External cheerfulness means that one's actions and behavior, which constitute one's external aspect, should always be upbeat and cheerful. This is completely incompatible with dejection, because a dejected person cannot even put on an act of being cheerful.

The concept of *lev shavur*, or a broken heart, is not the same as sadness. As one chassidic master said, there is nothing as whole as a broken heart.

A person who wins a large sum of money because he has six of the seven correct numbers on a lottery ticket is certainly happy about his good fortune, yet he cannot but feel that if he had only had the seventh number as well, he could have retired for life!

The infinite amount of Torah one can learn, and the depth of devotion and *kavanah* (concentration) wherewith one can fulfill *mitzvos* are so vast, that although a person can rejoice over his opportunity to serve G-d in this way, he can also realize how much better his Torah and *mitzvos* could be, and he can dedicate himself to enhancing and improving his service of G-d. Far from the paralyzing resignation that is characteristic of dejection, the "broken heart" attitude of not yet having done enough is an ongoing stimulus to personal growth, and since spiritual growth is the ultimate purpose of one's existence, this type of broken-heartedness is completely compatible with *simchah*.

You and your family should therefore share in the joy of the opportunity to fulfill Torah and *mitzvos,* and find many "kosher" ways in which to have cheerful experiences.

Correspondence 27

. . . I have been in *chinuch* for the past nine years, teaching *Chumash* and Gemara in fifth and sixth grades. Generally I think I have been doing well, and I was getting *sipuk* (gratification) from my work.

Last year I had a very weak class. Out of the eighteen children, perhaps four were good students. By pitching the level of learning towards the majority of the class, the few good students suffered. The class was a bust in all ways. The poor students accomplished little because they were unable to do better, and the good students accomplished little because they were not given enough. I discussed this with the principal, who told me to do the best I could.

The parents of all the students were very unhappy, and this affected me very deeply. I began to seriously question my abilities as a teacher. In their dissatisfaction they complained to the principal, who did not give me the support I expected.

This year I have a much better class, but I have a defeatist attitude. I think that perhaps I should leave *chinuch* and look for other areas of employment. This is not easy to do with a family to support, but I don't see fulfilling myself or succeeding in *chinuch*.

Your life's work is far too serious a matter to be dealt with by correspondence, and I am going to suggest that you discuss this much more thoroughly with a competent counselor.

However, there are several points that I do wish to address. There is no question that when you have a class of high achievers and you can observe their progress and receive the accolades of appreciative parents, this is extremely uplifting. Conversely, when you have a group of low achievers and receive unpleasant comments from dissatisfied parents, it is very distressful.

Yet, a person must be a *maven* on himself, and the impact of critical comments should not be devastating. The knowledge that you are a competent teacher should provide some insulation against the impact of critical comments.

There are people who have a need to prove themselves. Because of their self-doubts and low self-esteem, they need their egos strengthened and confirmed by demonstrable successful achievements. The fact is that this feeling of low self-esteem never actually leaves them, and it is only superficially alleviated by successful accomplishments. On the other hand, an unsuccessful outcome penetrates to their very core and aggravates their self-doubt.

It may be that the classes you taught until last year gave you an opportunity to prove your competence and self-worth. The problem is that there should have been no need to prove anything to yourself. You should have a self-concept that is not contingent on successful results in your work.

We should realize that our responsibility is to do as good a job as we possibly can. Of course, we must not be derelict in our work, we must always seek to improve our skills, and we must be dedicated to do the best we can. However, the outcome of our work is not in our hands. I can tell you from the medical aspect that excellent physicians who provide the finest treatment may have unfortunate outcomes. There are many factors that are not under our command, and we can therefore not control results. This is as true of teaching as it is of surgery.

If you have been functioning with a sense of low self-esteem, and were coasting along on the successful achievements of your students which compensated for your feelings of low self-esteem, then you were essentially courting distress, and it was only a matter of time before the inevitable happened: a class which did not provide you with an opportunity to vindicate yourself.

It is unfortunate that your principal did not provide you with the support you deserved, but even that is not the central issue. Much more important is that you must develop a sense of competence and worthiness which is not contingent on things beyond your control, such as the outcome of your efforts. Unless you do so, the same disappointments you had in *chinuch* can occur in every other profession or in business. No one has one hundred per cent success in anything, and where there is a strong element of self doubt, any outcome that is less than successful will reduce one's self-esteem and result in the depression such as you are now experiencing.

In the opening chapters of this book I expounded a bit on the statement by the Rabbi of Kotzk, "If I am I," etc. Just as one's identity should not be contingent on the opinion of others, neither should it be contingent on events beyond one's control.

I have been impressed with the effectiveness of the approach of "cognitive therapy" in helping overcome problems such as yours. Appended to this letter are the names of several therapists in your area, who I think are excellent in providing the necessary help.

If you have an interest in *chinuch*, it would be a disservice to the field if you were to leave it. I would suggest delaying any such decision until you have had adequate opportunity to have an evaluation and some therapy in self-esteem enhancement.

Correspondence 28

 . . . Both my wife and I never had much trust in psychologists, but we have read some of your books, especially *Living Each Day*, which has become a regular ritual of our day, and I think you may be able to direct me.

I have been married for ten years, and I have a college education with a bachelor's degree. I am now in my fifth business venture, and the first four were all failures. There seems to be a pattern in all this. The initial idea appears to be a good one, and the business starts off well, but after a few months it begins to sputter and go downhill. The same thing has occurred four times, and I am now in the first stage of my fifth business, and I guess I am expecting it to flop the way the others did.

I cannot fathom what I am doing wrong. I think I've just had a string of bad luck. But my wife thinks it may be something I am doing wrong that causes the failures. This does not make any sense to me, because I certainly want to succeed.

Maybe it is just not *bashert* (predestined) for me to succeed in business, and I should just stop trying. What do you recommend?

My first recommendation is to consult someone familiar with business. There are any number of business consultants available. Furthermore, there are many people who were successful in business and who are now retired, and would just love to become actively involved in a consultant capacity, and even participate in the operation of a business. There is no substitute for experience.

Insofar as success or failure may be predestined, this is no reason for not trying to do things right. If a person has done everything in the best possible way, yet does not succeed, there may be justification for one to say, "This was not meant to be." Even then, this does not preclude trying something else. The predestination may have been that one would not succeed in selling item "a," but may well succeed in selling item "b." However, if one is not conducting the business properly, there is no grounds to attribute its failure to predestination. The Torah says that "G-d will bless you in all the ventures that you do" (*Deuteronomy* 14:29), and implicit in "that you do" is doing it properly.

While there is certainly a possibility that one may unwittingly do things that undermine the success of a project, this should not be the first approach. For example, I have not been successful in maintaining plants in my home, and although I have never bought any, I have received a number of plants as gifts. The story is always the same: despite my always watering them according to instructions, they have a short life span and then wither. If it were really important for me to know plants, I would call in a horticulturist for guidance. I would not consult a psychologist on the assumption that I am subconsciously sabotaging the plants' survival.

Yet it is true that there are some people who consciously try to make a venture succeed, and unconsciously undermine it. People with low self-esteem may have a fear that a successful project would bring with it increasing responsibilities, and because of their feelings of inadequacy, they may be apprehensive about assuming the responsibilities. Also, people with low self-esteem, who feel they do not deserve to succeed, may actually have a sense of relief when something they have undertaken fails.

In my book, *When Do the Good Things Start?*, there is a cartoon where Charlie Brown says, "Some days you get up in the morning knowing you're going to do something stupid, and at the breakfast table you forget you're not having pancakes, and you pour syrup over your cold cereal. Well, it's good to get it over with." This kind of reaction is not uncommon, although it is often so subtle that the person is not aware of it, and although one may precipitate a failure, one attributes it to other causes.

If this is the only area of life where you seem to have a problem, I suggest you follow the first recommendation. If there are problems other than business, then therapy may be advisable. Should you need a referral, you may contact my office for the names of some psychotherapists in your area.

Correspondence 29

We are a *baal teshuvah* family, having become observant about ten years ago. My husband is a dentist, and while we are by no means wealthy, we are not hurting financially.

My father's parents were orthodox, and at age sixteen he rebelled and rejected all *Yiddishkeit,* and is very anti-religion. He was very upset with us when we became observant, and at every opportunity lets us know how terrible Orthodox Jews are.

We live some distance from my parents. Our phone conversations are polite, more like a cold war than peaceful coexistence. We visit for a few days twice a year, and you could cut the tension with a knife. Our last visit was particularly unpleasant, with my father's diatribe on our lifestyle and how destructive we are to our children by sending them to an Orthodox day school.

Last year I went to some classes where the rabbi lectured on *middos* (character traits) and said that anger is a terrible trait that must be eradicated. But I cannot stop myself for feeling angry at the way my father treats me.

To make things worse, we would like to buy a new home. My father could easily help us, but I hesitate to ask him, because if he refuses, I would feel even more angry, which is wrong. I feel terribly guilty about how I feel.

Anger is probably the most difficult emotion to deal with, and the improper management of anger is at the root of many symptoms, both psychologic and physical. Many people have difficulty with anger, totally apart from religious scruples. They may feel that being angry threatens a relationship, and if they are involved in a dependent relationship, they may repress their anger out of fear that feeling or showing their anger will jeopardize their source of support.

Judaism does have much to say about anger, but some of what it teaches has unfortunately been distorted.

Anger is an emotion over which one has no control. If someone provokes you, you will feel anger. Inasmuch as feeling anger is beyond control, you cannot be at fault for feeling it. What you *do* in response to a provocation, or how you *react* to anger is indeed under your control, and one's reaction can be morally good or bad.

It is noteworthy that the Talmud states, "Someone who breaks things in a fit of rage is committing a grave sin" (*Shabbos* 105b). Thus, it is not the feeling that is condemned, but the acting out of the feeling. Striking out, whether physically or verbally, is sinful, but *feeling* anger is not. If the one who provokes is a parent, one should be most cautious so that one does not transgress the commandment requiring respect of parents. But again, it is the reaction rather than the feeling that must be controlled.

King Solomon (*Ecclesiastes* 7:9) states that "Anger rests in the bosom of a fool." By that he means that a wise person who is provoked to anger will find ways to dissipate the feeling, whereas the fool will continue to harbor resentments. Again, it is not the arousal of anger that is wrong, but the retention of it after it could have been dissipated.

Dissipation of anger, contrary to what some say, does not mean hitting a punching bag while imagining that it is the object of one's anger. There is no indication that this is of any psychological value. Rather, one can allow the anger to dissipate by understanding how and why the provoker acted.

In your situation, although we do not know for certain why your father developed an antagonism towards religion, we may hazard a guess that in the absence of day schools when he was a child, he probably had to attend after school Talmud Torah in order to prepare for his bar mitzvah. While his classmates were enjoying themselves with sports activities, he had to sit in a classroom after a full day of school, learning how to read a language which he was never helped to understand, in order to be able to recite a few paragraphs on the Saturday nearest his thirteenth birthday, so that his parents could throw a party to impress their friends. Torah observance might have been presented to him in a very authoritarian manner, without any understanding of it whatever, and often with gross inconsistencies if not frank hypocrisy. People who grew up in such an environment relate how bitter they felt toward religion.

Yet, for all his anger at religion, his deviating from the parents' lifestyle probably did not occur without generating guilt feelings, which he may have sought to mitigate by ridiculing religious observance as archaic and obsolete. These feelings of guilt may have been greatly intensified when his children picked up what he had discarded. Without justifying your father's behavior, it is not too difficult to understand why he reacted at age sixteen, and again at age sixty-six.

While your father's critical remarks undoubtedly hurt you and elicit a feeling of anger toward him, your understanding of why he may be reacting in this way should help you to rid yourself of this anger. Note that I did not say that it would *prevent* you from becoming angry, but rather that it should help you dispose of the anger after the event.

As an intern, I recall being struck in the face by a diabetic patient who suffered an insulin reaction and who had no control whatever of his actions. Although this person was not responsible for his behavior, the sharp pain I felt aroused a feeling of anger. After the acute pain subsided, I was able to dispose of the anger by realizing that he was not responsible for his actions, but this did not prevent the feeling of anger from initially occurring.

When your father's remarks hurt you, they arouse anger, and this you cannot control. After a bit, you should realize why he may have acted in this way, and the anger can then dissipate. This is what Solomon meant: A wise person will learn how to rid oneself of anger, whereas a fool will retain it.

Although a person cannot eliminate the arousal of anger within him by his own efforts, that does not mean that it can never be eliminated. One may pray to G-d to be relieved of this feeling, and G-d can do for us what we cannot do for ourselves.

Asking G-d to remove anger before we have made a maximum effort to restrain our responses and to dissipate it as explained above is certainly inappropriate. G-d's answer would be, "Go do your homework first." However, even after one has made a dedicated and sincere effort to manage anger properly, there is no guarantee that G-d will remove it. It may be His will, for reasons known only to Him, that one continue to battle with it. Character growth occurs only with struggle, and if one's request to be relieved of all anger is not fulfilled, it may be because one still has additional growing to do.

Insofar as asking your father for financial help, I see nothing wrong with it. As a rule, parents enjoy giving to their children. If he happens to be in a state of mind wherein he refuses your request, this disappointment may arouse anger within you, but you should then deal with it as mentioned above.

Correspondence 30

. . . I am twenty-two, single, with a degree in education.

I have had an interest in psychology, and have the time and financial means to pursue a degree in psychology. My questions are: (1) Are the teachings in psychology something to which a *frum* woman should be exposed? (2) Would I be able to weed out which concepts in psychology are compatible with Torah and which are not? (3) What effect would going for a doctorate have on arranging a *shidduch* (matrimonial match) with a true *ben Torah* (Torah scholar)?

I believe there is a great need for Torah-observant women in psychology. I am regularly consulted by Orthodox women who are in need of psychologic treatment or counseling, and many of them would best be served by a female psychotherapist who is familiar with and can empathize with the problems of a

Torah-observant woman. There are various problems within marriage and in child-rearing that may not be fully understood either by a male therapist or a non-Orthodox female therapist. As there are a few Orthodox female therapists, there is certainly a void to be filled.

The exposure to psychological theories that conflict with Torah should not be a threat. You are already exposed to more detrimental ideas in the printed and audio-visual media, some of which may even appeal to one's sense of propriety. There are two opinions in the Talmud about the angel of Esau that wrestled with Jacob (*Genesis* 32:25). One says that he had the appearance of a pagan idolater, and the other says he had the appearance of a *talmid chacham* (Torah scholar). Ideas that are antagonistic to Torah may appear overtly as such or may take on a cloak of righteousness. We must always be on our guard against being duped, and our only defense is to present these ideas before an authentic Torah scholar to pass on their validity. This can be applied to psychological theories as well.

While there are a number of concepts in psychology that are incompatible with Torah, there are many others that are not only compatible with Torah philosophy, but can actually be found in Torah literature. Some traditional psychological concepts, such as those of some psychoanalysts are essentially only of historical interest, and have largely been replaced by behaviorist and cognitive schools. Yet, there is much that can be salvaged even from psychoanalytic psychology, such as unconscious motivation or the system of psychological defenses. The fact that the Torah holds a person responsible for *shogeg* acts (inadvertent sinful act) indicates that a person is responsible for behavior even when not completely conscious of it. There is a wealth of psychology in *Mesillas Yesharim (Path of the Just)* and *Tanya*, and it is indeed unfortunate that we often remain unaware of these treasures until we rediscover them only after studying psychology. Had we been *zocheh* (deserving), we could have discovered them at the source.

There is a possibility that obtaining a degree in psychology may narrow your options for a *shidduch*. Some *bnei Torah* who do not have a college education may be concerned that a woman in possession of a degree might look down upon them. While there are a number of fine *bnei Torah* with advanced secular degrees, they are, of course, fewer in number.

On the other hand, I know several couples where the husbands are fine *talmidei chachamim,* who did not attend college, and whose wives have an advanced secular education, and whose marriages are excellent. In these cases both the husbands and wives have a profound respect for Torah, and neither spouse considers the wife's college degree to in any way diminish the husband's stature.

In at least some cases, the inference is that those *bnei Torah* who do think that a wife's secular degree would be a threat to them are lacking in self-esteem, and are actually underestimating their Torah scholarship. If they felt more secure in their status as *talmidei chachamim,* perhaps they would not consider a secular education to be in any way threatening. By self-esteem I do not mean that they should consider themselves to be the greatest Torah scholars in existence, because that would be *gahvah* (vanity), but rather that as serious students of Torah there is no reason for them to feel inferior to someone with an advanced secular education. I believe that their fear that the *wife* may consider them inferior is nothing but a projection of their own feelings.

Best wishes for *hatzlachah* in whatever you do.

Correspondence 31

. . .I come from a very fine Torah-observant family, and last year I met a young woman who is also from a respectable, professional, observant family. I am 28, she is 24. For some reason, my parents took a dislike to her from the beginning. Because of my parents' opposition, we broke off for several months, but we renewed our relationship and we wish to get married.

My parents are beside themselves. They point out faults in her which I do not see, and they say that I am blinded by passion and am entering a destructive relationship. My family says it will kill my father if I marry her.

I am between a rock and a hard place. I know that halachah does not require me to defer to my parents' wishes, but I also do not wish to hurt them or to sever my relationship with them, which they have threatened to do if I marry her. I have consulted our rabbi, who states that he cannot provide me with any guidance. I suspect that he does not wish to antagonize my parents, who are influential members of his synagogue.

Is there any way I can get my parents to change their minds?

Without talking to your parents, I have no way of knowing what their objections are and whether they have any validity. It is, of course, possible that someone in love may indeed be oblivious to character defects which a more objective person can see, but it is also possible that their objections are emotional rather than rational, and have no basis in fact.

The only thing I can suggest is that you and the young woman consult someone who is qualified in couples' therapy. Prior to this interview you should inform the therapist of your parents' objection. The therapist may decide to see you both individually and together or only as a couple. In either case, the therapist will have the opportunity to evaluate each of you as well as the soundness of the relationship. A competent therapist is an objective observer, and is free of the bias of passion or any emotional antagonism.

If the therapist feels that your parents' objections are valid, you would be wise to re-evaluate the relationship, and perhaps continue to see the therapist to clarify your course of action. If the therapist finds that there is no validity to your parents' opposition, you can then arrange for your parents to meet with him/her. If your parents' objections should persist even after the therapist has pointed out their fallacies, then you must make what is the best decision for you.

Your options are then only two: (1) to proceed with the marriage and your parents either will or will not adjust to it, or (2) break off the relationship in deference to your parents' and family's wishes. The wording of the Torah, "Therefore shall a man leave his father and mother and cleave onto his wife" (*Genesis* 2:24)" seems to speak for itself.

There is yet another consideration. In the best and happiest of marriages there are some rough spots, and this is simply reality. In fantasy, no such rough spots need exist. If you terminate this relationship with someone whom you love, and later marry someone who meets with your parents' approval, you will always be comparing that relationship to the one you could have had. The second will be in reality, and cannot measure up to the one in fantasy. This is not only unwise for you, but grossly unfair to the woman you will marry, who will have to compete against a fantasy.

It is sometimes possible that parents may discourage a child's marriage because they are unable to let go, in which case they may find reasons to disapprove of everyone about whom their child is serious. I have no way of knowing whether this is a factor in your case. I mention it because I have seen it happen, and it is a severe mistake for children not to marry in order to provide companionship to their parents. All parents wish that their children survive them, and this is the way things are supposed to be. Making a contract with parents to be their companions is one which a parent cannot honor, and when he/she is gone the child is then left alone and forsaken.

I suggest you follow through with an adequate psychologic evaluation, to firstly put your mind at rest that you are not overlooking some significant factor, and secondly, that you will provide at least a valid, rational case to your parents.

Correspondence 32

... My son is fifteen, a rather big fifteen. He attends a yeshivah and is, thank G-d doing well. The reason for my concern is that in the past few months I have noted a change in him. I cannot really describe it accurately, but he is different. He used to talk with us much more, but now he keeps things to himself. When he is home from yeshivah he either reads or learns in his room, and does not communicate much with us or his younger brother and sister (he is the oldest). On Shabbos he does bring friends home, but it is his relationship with the family that appears awkward.

He is diligent in his learning, beginning the day early, and learns quite late at night. Perhaps he is not getting enough sleep for a young boy.

I don't know what to do, whether he should be talking to a psychiatrist, because something must be bothering him, but I don't want him to think he is not normal.

What do you suggest?

... Let me first state that I am not an adolescent psychiatrist, and I cannot speak as authoritatively about adolescents as about adults. Nevertheless, I will try to share some of my ideas with you.

Adolescence is a difficult period, and although most of humanity somehow survives this transition period, it is a period of increased vulnerability to emotional problems.

Parenthetically, adolescence as we know it is an invention of western civilization and not a natural phenomenon. Nature knows only pre-puberty and post-puberty, and the period of puberty itself is a rather brief one, corresponding approximately to the period recognized in halachah. From a halachic-legal aspect, a child is a minor until a specific moment, and on the event of the twelfth or thirteenth birthday, becomes an adult. There is a period of several months during which halachah recognizes a phase of puberty.

Puberty is physiologic, and while changes do continue to occur for a longer period of time, the period between being a physiologic minor and a physiologic adult is quite brief. Our ancestors were very much in concert with physiology when they married off their children at an early age.

Western civilization introduced the concept of adolescence, during which a person is no longer a minor, but not yet an adult. Instead of being in concert with physiology, adolescence has much more to do with social issues, especially one's earning capacity. Thus, in a culture where a person may not be self-supporting until one has a masters degree, which may not be achieved until perhaps age twenty-five, a person who is physiologically an adult at thirteen cannot anticipate becoming a "social" adult for another twelve years. This can be an extremely frustrating phase.

As a child becomes an adolescent, some very radical changes

occur both physiologically and emotionally, which can have pronounced psychological effects. Very powerful yearnings, which the youngster may find difficult to manage. The bodily changes may result in a rather awkward phase, which may make the youngster very self-conscious. It is not unusual for a youngster to think that he/she is the only one in the world that is experiencing these feelings. Communicating these feelings to someone might significantly alleviate this stress and sense of loneliness, but these are the kinds of feelings that are not easily shared, especially with parents. These youngsters may therefore tend to withdraw into themselves.

Since communicating these thoughts and feelings to parents is so difficult, it would be of great help if the youngster could confide in someone. A receptive, empathic teacher or counselor can be of enormous help.

Youngsters trying to cope with the stresses of adolescence may become desperate, and may be attracted to anything which promises to resolve their uncertainties. This is why they are so vulnerable to cults, drugs, and other social deviances at this age. Because they feel awkward in relating to their parents, they may try to "have some space."

In the modern secular world, the permissiveness that prevails encourages the youngsters to freely express or "experiment" with gratifying all their drives and emotions. This is not only unacceptable halachically, but is also psychologically unsound. The youngster who is guided by halachah may nevertheless need an empathic ear and an authority figure whom he/she can respect.

The behavior you describe in your son thus may be a normal adolescent phenomenon. The fact that he rises early in the morning, relates to friends, and can concentrate on Talmudic studies for long periods of time indicates that there is no reason for being alarmed that something of a very serious psychological nature is occurring.

However, because the adolescent is so vulnerable to rather extremely emotional reactions, it is important to remain alert. Adolescents may become depressed, over and above the usual mood swings characteristic of this period. They may detach themselves from friends and may not be able to concentrate on their studies. They may turn to a life of fantasy to escape the distress they are experiencing in reality.

Please be aware that your son's apparent avoidance of you is in no way an indication that he does not love you. Such a conclusion would be a serious mistake, and would only add to his stress. If he ever seems willing to talk, be sure to listen. You might also investigate whether there is someone in the yeshivah who knows how to approach adolescents who need a listening ear.

I do not see any urgent need to insist that he see a psychotherapist unless he expresses the desire to talk to someone. However, I think it would be very wise for you to consult someone with expertise in problems of adolescents to whom you could relate his behavior. This would accomplish two purposes, in that this person could provide guidance as to how to relate most constructively, and would also be able to help you detect if anything more serious should occur which would then require professional attention.

Correspondence 33

I am now thirty-four, married to a wonderful man, and we have two lovely children.

Very early in my marriage I did a very foolish and very terrible thing. After a few years, keeping this secret bottled up within me was destroying me, and I told my husband about it. He was deeply hurt, but said that he was pleased that I was frank with him, but that we would need an authoritative halachic opinion. The rabbi we consulted ruled that we could remain married.

Nevertheless, I am living in the torment of hell. I simply cannot forgive myself. My husband says he loves me and that he has forgiven me, but that does not alleviate the anguish. I often think of leaving the marriage, but why should I do this to my two children who love me and love their father, and I am a good mother to them. However, my guilt is so unrelenting that I don't know if my marriage is viable. I discussed my dilemma with my rabbi, who suggested that I see a psychiatrist. I did so for a few months, and in addition to my therapy sessions, he prescribed anti-depressant medicine. However, I did not feel any different.

I am turning to you because perhaps as a rabbi and a psychiatrist you may be able to save me. Please help.

Inasmuch as you are addressing your question to me as a rabbi as well as from a psychological aspect, there is something that must be clarified about halachah.

A halachic decision is not similar to a law enacted by a legislature or a legal decision rendered by a court. Halachah is Torah, and Torah must be understood to encompass both ethical values and psychological truths.

We sometimes read about "natural law" as being distinct from laws enacted by society. In halachah there is no such distinction. The *Midrash* states that the Torah is the "blueprint" according to which G-d created the world. This means that Torah law *is* the natural law. Hence, a halachic ruling cannot be incompatible with natural law.

If a secular court rejects a suit for divorce, that says nothing about the viability of the marriage. When halachah rules that a marriage may continue, that does not of course mean that the marriage *must* continue, but that it is viable. If one feels guilty for having transgressed the Torah, and if it is this type of guilt that is threatening the marriage, then one must realize that there must be some misperception of the concept of guilt. Since halachah encompasses natural law, it would not condone a marriage which is non-viable. While there may be other reasons for dissolving a marriage, the type of healthy guilt that results from a violation of Torah should not be the reason, else halachah would not have ruled the marriage to be viable.

What is healthy guilt? It is a painful feeling resulting from having done something wrong. It is akin to physical pain resulting from an injury or a disease. Without physical pain, a person might sustain serious harm without being aware of it, or die as a result of a painless ruptured appendix. Physical pain deters one from exposing oneself to harm, and alerts one that there is something wrong with the way the body is functioning.

Healthy guilt results from an improper action. It is a distressful feeling that deters us from committing improper acts, because we do not wish to bear the consequent guilt. If one has done something improper, guilt is then the motivating force that leads one to atone and make whatever amends are called for, as well as to alert one not to repeat the act. Healthy guilt is not in the domain of psychotherapy. It does not require "treatment" because it is not a disease. Needless to say, healthy guilt should not be medicated with tranquilizers.

For the Jew, the standard of proper and improper acts is the Torah, and awareness of transgression of the Torah should generate healthy guilt.

Just as we are told that the Torah is the "blueprint" whereby G-d created the world, we are also told that *teshuvah* (repentance) preceded the creation of the world. In other words, the concept of *teshuvah*, which is contained in the Torah, is part of natural law. Proper *teshuvah* can therefore alleviate healthy guilt and allow a person to live free of the burden of one's mistakes.

If guilt persists after one has done *teshuvah,* there are only two possible explanations: (1) The *teshuvah* was not adequate, and (2) the guilt was not healthy guilt. We do know psychologically that just as there may be physical pain in the absence of any evident injury or disease, there can also be unwarranted guilt. The latter is a problem which is indeed in the domain of the psychologist.

What constitutes proper *teshuvah?* Regret for having done wrong and a sincere determination not to repeat the act are primary. If the transgression affected someone else negatively, it is essential to make appropriate restitution wherever possible and to ask forgiveness from the person offended. But while these are primary, they do not yet constitute complete *teshuvah.*

The *Rambam* (Maimonides) states that *teshuvah* is achieved when "the One Who knows all innermost thoughts will testify that the person will not repeat the act." This statement has caused some commentaries to ask, inasmuch as a person always has freedom of choice and G-d does not interfere with actions that are subject to free will, how can the *Rambam* say that G-d will testify that the person will never repeat an act? We might also wonder why the *Rambam* chose to use the Divine attribute of "the One Who knows all inner-most thoughts." If indeed the Divine testimony is that the person will never repeat the act, it would have been more appropriate to list the Divine attribute as "the One Who foresees the future."

We must understand that a sin does not occur in a vacuum. A person commits a particular sin only because he was in a spiritual state wherein that sin could occur. For example, a man who rises at dawn, recites *Tehillim (Psalms)*, goes to *mikvah* and prays with a *minyan,* is quite unlikely to stop at a fast-food restaurant and have *treifah* (non-kosher) sausage for breakfast. This is simply incompatible with his spiritual state.

The awareness that one has committed a sin should therefore lead one to the conclusion that one had been spiritually deficient, and this deficiency enabled the particular act to occur. It is therefore not sufficient that one regret the act and resolve not to repeat it. Even sincere regret and resolution will not prevent a recurrence. One must make a careful analysis of how and why the act occurred, and do those things that will correct the deficiency and elevate one to a level of spirituality wherein such an act cannot possibly occur.

A person who would never think of eating *treifah,* and who discovers that he spoke *lashon hara* (slander or gossip) must work on his spiritual perfection so that *lashon hara* becomes as unthinkable an act as eating *treifah.* Anything less than that is an incomplete *teshuvah* for committing the sin of speaking *lashon hara.*

This is clearly the *Rambam*'s intent when he describes true *teshuvah.* He is not saying that G-d, "Who foresees the future," will testify that the person will not repeat the act. This is not a prediction. Rather, it is that G-d, *Who knows one's innermost thoughts,* will attest that this person has advanced himself to a level of spirituality wherein that particular act is no longer feasible. Should that individual regress and descend to a lower level of spirituality, he may indeed repeat the act, but if, at his current level of spirituality, such an act is unfeasible, then his *teshuvah* is complete.

Whatever you did occurred because you were in a spiritual state which permitted such an occurrence. If you have brought yourself to a state where this can no longer occur, then your *teshuvah* is complete.

When true *teshuvah* has been attained, one must totally detach oneself from the sinful act. One must accept the Divine assurance, "I have erased your sin like a fog that has dispersed" (*Isaiah* 44:22). Just as when a fog clears no trace of it remains, so when one has done proper *teshuvah,* one must have faith that G-d has erased the sin. To obsess on the sin is a serious mistake. Indeed, the Rabbi of Kotzk said that inasmuch as the essence of a person is one's mind, wherever one's mind is, that is where the person is. If one reflects upon the sin, one is back into it.

But if one is to totally detach from the sin and not reflect on it, why does the Psalmist say, "My sin is always before me" (*Psalms* 51:5). This would seem to require constant focusing on the sin, which we have just indicated is not desirable.

The Hebrew word for "sin," *chet*, also means a lack or a defect. Inasmuch as a sin can occur, as we have said, only in the presence of a spiritual defect that renders the person vulnerable to the sin, it is this spiritual defect that the person had that one must be aware of, rather than the sinful act itself. The reason one must be aware of this defect is that inasmuch as it was once there, one is at the risk of reverting into that state, and if one has advanced spiritually, one must take proper precaution to avoid spiritual relapse. In the very same Psalm, David asks G-d to let him experience joy and gladness (51:10). This would be impossible if one were to be constantly pre-occupied with one's sin, which would lead to a state of morbid dejection. It is clear that after proper *teshuvah* has been effected, one must abandon the sin itself, and that the attention should be focused on maintaining one's advanced spiritual level.

Not all people are alike in their emotional composition and temperaments. The intensity of physical drives and appetites varies from individual to individual. A person must be aware of his areas of vulnerability and reinforce himself against a lapse in that particular area.

The *Rambam* recommends adopting "the mean of virtue"; i.e., avoiding extremes and following an intermediate path; e.g., judicious courage rather than cowardliness at the one pole and fool-hardy recklessness at the other. Yet he also states that just as a bent twig may have to be bent in the opposite direction in order to straighten it, so there may be a necessity to move more towards one pole in order to counteract a particular weakness.

Our environment is saturated with provocative stimuli. Morals have sunk to an all-time low, and the most explicit obscenity is displayed openly. Brute animals are not as degenerate as some segments of modern society have become. While provocative stimuli should be shunned by every moral person, someone who has fallen prey to a moral indiscretion must exercise additional caution and make extra effort to avoid provocative stimuli, whether in the media, literature, or public displays. Needless to say, the Torah concepts of avoiding proscribed physical contact should be meticulously observed, and one must be continuously wary of associations, such as may occur socially or occupationally.

One more aspect deserves mention. We may have difficulty conceptualizing ideas that are not within our personal experience. One may wonder, how is it possible for G-d to totally erase a sin even after I have done *teshuvah*? After all, an act is a factual reality. Can reality be undone?

The level of forgiveness one can accept corresponds to the level of forgiveness one has experienced. If someone has offended me, and I claim to have forgiven him, yet continue to harbor a resentment of him, I have not experienced total forgiveness and therefore cannot conceive how G-d can forgive *me*. It is only when I can understand that the offense against me was committed in a particular emotional or stressed condition, and that the person has sincerely apologized and no longer wishes me harm, and on the basis of that I totally extirpate any and all resentments towards that person, that I can then understand how G-d can forgive me.

The Talmud states that one merits Divine forgiveness according to the degree with which one forgives others. In addition to this being in keeping with the concept of *middah keneged middah*, G-d acting towards us as we act towards other, it also has a psychological basis. We can accept forgiveness only to the extent we experience it when we forgive others.

I hope this clarifies some of your problems, and I will be glad to respond to any future questions on these issues.

Correspondence 34

I am writing to you because your book, *Let Us Make Man,* was an important stimulus to me when I became a *baal teshuvah* over a year ago.

We are a third generation Reform family. My parents are very much involved with Israel, and my mother is an officer in Hadassah. We live in a Midwest city where there is very little *Yiddishkeit.*

During my senior year in high school, with plans to enter college — but with no definite career in mind — I began searching for something more than what I was seeing in my family. They are lovely people who are charitable, but their goal in life appears to be to make more money than the next person, and to tell everyone about the expensive vacations they had. It just seemed to me to be such an empty existence. I went to New York to an NCSY Shabbaton, and a new world opened up. I began to read everything I could about *Yiddishkeit.*

When I made my decision to go to a yeshivah after high school, my parents thought I had flipped. To their credit, they did not try to stop me. My father, who tends to be cynical, said, "Go ahead. You're young and you have the time to experiment. You'll find that it's all show and that they are no different than we are, then you'll come back and take life seriously."

I went to a *baal teshuvah* yeshivah in New York. There was a lot I liked, but it seemed to me that too many *frum* people, even though they keep Shabbos and kosher, really don't have goals that are much more spiritual than my family's. I then decided to attend a *baal teshuvah* yeshivah in Israel. I suppose I was naive. I really did not expect to see angels in human dress, but I have been disappointed.

For example, in your book you say that Torah observance can provide people with self-esteem so that they should not have to emulate other people to overcome feelings of unworthiness. I just don't see that this is true. You list the Torah values of being satisfied with whatever one has, not seeking power over anyone, giving honor instead of receiving it, and accepting teaching from everyone. Why, then, are so many who claim to be Torah observant people not satisfied with what they have? Our Rebbe told us that the Chafetz Chaim would close his store in the morning as soon as he had earned enough for that day. I don't see anyone even remotely thinking that way, let alone doing it. I don't see many people humbling themselves to learn from others. To the contrary, everybody seems to think they are the wisest.

The politics here has been absolutely disgusting, and the Torah observant are in the thick of it. They seem to be preoccupied with having the power and control, and no one thinks it is more important to give honor than to receive it.

There should be happiness if one is following the will of G-d as expressed in the Torah, but I don't see all that many happy people. Every family seems to have its problems and miseries. The orthodox are not going around humming a happy tune all day.

My father's words ring in my ears. I have not decided to go back, and perhaps it's my pride that doesn't let me admit that he was right. One of the things my father was afraid of is that my younger brother, who always worshipped me as his hero, would follow in my footsteps. I don't think that as of now I would encourage him to do so.

Maybe the goal in life is not to take expensive vacations, and learning Torah is a wonderful thing, but I see too many people mouthing Torah and doing whatever they please, except that they don't transgress the Shabbos and they eat kosher.

The infighting among observant people is loathsome. Some of the people I respect the most are those who are willing to live with the bare necessities of life in the new settlements, because they believe in settling the land. They are also the ones who seem to be the most content. They learn Torah, and keep kosher and many have beards. But the major Torah scholars here look upon them as second-class citizens. It is all very confusing to me.

Because your book had an important part in my becoming a *baal teshuvah,* I hope you can take some time to answer me. If you are ever in Israel, I would like to meet you.

 Let me begin with a quote from the Talmud. Rabbi Shimon bar Yochai said, "I have seen people who have attained an exalted spiritual level, and they are very few" (*Sukkah* 45b). He goes on to say that in his generation there may be as few as two people who merit that description, even though there were many Torah scholars and observant people in his time. Yet, Rabbi Shimon did not see this as a failure of Torah. Rather, he was adamant in his repudiation of the secular world and its hedonism (which resulted in his being hunted by the Roman authorities) and proceeded to write the Zohar, to make spirituality more accessible to everyone.

G-d created the world and initially populated it with one person. This, the Talmud tells us, serves to indicate that one person can be an entire world. If among the billions of people in the world there is only one person who achieves the spiritual level that G-d desires, this may suffice.

If all the Torah teaching resulted in the production of only one

Chafetz Chaim, that is an achievement to be proud of. The secular world has never produced even one Chafetz Chaim, nor anyone even remotely comparable to him.

But for all his greatness, the Chafetz Chaim was far from an isolated phenomenon. His generation was rich in *tzaddikim* that were truly highly spiritual people, and this is certainly true of the generations that preceded him. Some of these great people were recognized for their enormous stature, while countless others remained unknown.

One of the basic characteristics of the Torah personality is *anivus* (humility). Those *gedolei haTorah* (great Torah personalities) that are known to us assumed positions of leadership because, like Moses, it was their responsibility to their people. Innumerable others remain unknown to us to this very day.

Just in the last generation, there was a proprietor of a hardware store, Reb Menachem Zemba, who was an inordinate Torah scholar, but no one knew of this. At one point the Rabbi of Gur insisted that he come out of concealment because his people needed him. We have no idea how many *tzaddikim* and Torah scholars were permitted to retain their low profile.

The disaster of the Holocaust robbed us of so many of our great Torah personalities, and we are far from recouping this terrible loss. Yet, in our own generation, we were fortunate to see individuals who lived full Torah lives with true Torah values, such as the Chazon Ish, HaGaon Reb Moshe Feinstein, HaGaon Reb Aharon Kotler, HaGaon Rav Yaakov Kamenetsky, the Steipler Gaon, to name just a few. The secular world may have its scientists, artists, and philosophers, but it does not produce personalities of this caliber.

The six hundred and thirteen *mitzvos* of the Torah are the building blocks of a spiritual life, without which a Jew cannot achieve the goals and purpose which G-d has established. However, it is possible that a person may have all the building blocks and not assemble them into a structure. The plans for the structure are the great ethical works such as *Mesilas Yesharim (Path of the Just)*, *Chovos HaLevavos (Duties of the Heart)*, and others.

Some people may have assembled only part of the structure,

others more, and some may have completed it. It is true that some may have a pile of building blocks and have not yet built any structure. Nevertheless, having the building blocks enables them to do so, and they may be stimulated to get to work assembling them, but without the building blocks, one has no chance at all.

One may be disillusioned if one sees a person, whose appearance labels him as observant, behaving in a manner that is in frank violation of the Torah laws that dictate proper behavior in commerce and in relating to other people. There is no justification for this, and corrupt behavior, whether public or private, is to be soundly condemned. Yet, one must not fall into the trap of judging the group by the behavior of a few individuals, or even many individuals.

The ideals of Torah are available to you. They are beautiful and eternal. Today's secular world with its lack of absolute morals has degenerated to a decadence unknown since the legendary nadir of Sodom. You may find people in the Torah world who do not shape up to Torah standards, but this is a reflection on them as individuals, and not on the Torah.

The fact that not all Torah-observant people are walking around humming a merry tune is in no way a shortcoming of Torah observance. You will recall that Adam was expelled from *Gan Eden* (Paradise), and that man was thereafter condemned to a life of struggle. On this earth, there is no paradise, and there is unfortunately an abundance of suffering.

In his classic work, *Derech Hashem (The Way of G-d)*, Luzzato states that life is meant to be a series of trials and ordeals, which man must withstand. This must be so according to the Divine system of justice, and in order to fulfill the Divine plan. The ultimate reason for this is beyond human comprehension, and there is the unanswerable question as to why virtuous people are subject to such great distress. The Talmud states that when Moses sought to understand why this is so, G-d told him that no living being can fathom this. Indeed, one Talmudic opinion ascribes the authorship of the *Book of Job* to Moses. In *Job* the question why the virtuous suffer is elaborately discussed, and the final conclusion is that it is beyond our understanding.

Indeed, it is possible for those who are most spiritual to be subject to the greatest stresses. We are told that G-d does not burden a person with a greater trial than one can withstand. This means that the more spiritual a person becomes, the more he can withstand the severity of the trial, hence the more vulnerable he becomes to such a trial.

In *Ethics of the Fathers* (5:4) we are taught that the patriarch Abraham was subjected to ten trials of progressively increasing severity, and that he withstood them all, which shows us Abraham's intense love for G-d. We might ask, this indeed teaches Abraham's fortitude and loyalty, but how is this an indication of his love for G-d?

However, we can now understand that as the Patriarch advanced in his spirituality, he thereby rendered himself subject to ever greater trials. After the first few, Abraham certainly recognized the pattern, and knew that if he continued his spiritual growth, he would be opening himself to even greater distresses. Someone of lesser mettle might have stopped, and have settled for whatever spiritual level one had achieved, and would not have invited greater distress. Abraham's love of G-d was so great that he continued to bring himself closer to G-d, knowing full well that he might have to experience increasing suffering.

Spiritual people are thus subject to severe distress, and it is unrealistic to expect them to be constantly manifesting great joy. There are, however, many spiritual people who are able to experience *simchah* at appropriate occasions, albeit their life situation is such that others in that state could not possibly rise above their grief and suffering and experience joy. Our great *tzaddikim* were indeed able to be joyous while suffering, and many accepted their suffering with *simchah*. While one may not be able to expect this attitude from those who have not reached such spiritual heights, the very fact that they can be joyous at all is a remarkable achievement.

We review the biographies of our *tzaddikim*, not because they are interesting stories, but because they show us the capabilities of a human being, and to what levels of spirituality a person can rise. It is within everyone's reach to achieve spirituality through Torah.

Can you become a Chafetz Chaim? Before you totally rule this out, bear in mind that many people who believe this is beyond anyone's capacity are not at all unlikely to buy a lottery ticket. Mathematically, the chances of becoming a Chafetz Chaim are greater than winning the lottery. Perhaps one is more hopeful about the lottery because it requires no effort, while becoming a Chafetz Chaim requires a great deal of effort.

May you be blessed with success in Torah growth.

Correspondence 35

I am twenty-eight, happily married to an Orthodox rabbi, and we live in a town with a rather small Jewish community. We have two children, ages three and five.

When I was seventeen, I became bulemic. I don't know what caused the onset of the condition. The only thing I can think of is that when I was a child I was short and heavy, and the kids used to call me "fatty." I don't recall that bothering me very much. At about thirteen I grew taller and slimmed down, and food was not a problem. At seventeen I began bingeing and then starving myself to keep my weight down. Since I was away from home at school, nobody paid any attention as to whether I ate or not. When I came home for vacation, my parents did not detect anything. When I said that I just did not feel like eating, they accepted this at face value. I was doing well at school, and they had no cause for concern. On only a few occasions did I force myself to regurgitate what I had eaten.

I was married at twenty-one, and I was sure that marriage would solve my problem. I tried very hard not to binge, so that I would not have to starve myself and raise my husband's suspicions. The few times I did binge I was able to get away with skipping meals and exercising like crazy. I dreaded my husband discovering my craziness. I love him very much and he worships the ground I walk on. No woman could ask for a better husband.

When I became pregnant I could do as I wished, because everything is attributed to the strange eating habits of pregnancy. After delivery I was thirty pounds heavier than normal, but no one cared. Within two years I was expecting again and my secret was again safe. I added twenty additional pounds. I gained another twenty pounds during the year I nursed my baby.

I was now at 175 pounds, and I hated myself. I tried all kinds of magic diets but nothing worked. My life became one of great misery. I cried frequently, and my husband tried to console me that he didn't care how much I weighed, that he loved me anyway. But could anyone love me when I hated myself? I became desperate and started to force myself to throw up.

I finally broke down and told my husband that he was married to a crazy woman. I told him I had been like this before he married me, and that if he didn't want to stay married to me I could understand. He still doesn't realize how sick I am. But I am terribly depressed and I might have even done away with myself if it weren't for those two lovable kids.

Then I heard a talk show about people like myself who were going to Overeaters Anonymous. I went without telling my husband, and when I did tell him what it was like he was very concerned that it was a non-Jewish religious organization and he didn't want me to go. Now I don't know what to do. The one thing I know is that I cannot go on like this.

I came across an article of yours in an Anglo-Jewish paper, and I traced you down. What, if anything, can I do to get out of this terrible rut?

In order to properly address your problem, I might have to write a textbook on eating disorders, which I cannot do now. Let me just touch on a few highlights.

I will begin with your last point. Overeaters Anonymous (O.A.) is an adaptation of Alcoholics Anonymous (A.A.) to problems of eating disorders. Although the A.A. program had its origin with people who were devout Christians, the program itself, i.e., the twelve steps of A.A. or O.A., are not in any way incompatible with Jewish philosophy or halachah. It is true that group meetings are most often held in churches, but this is primarily because they have not been invited into synagogues. Although most meetings close with the recitation of the Lord's Prayer, this is not an integral part of the program, and anyone is free to say (or not say) any prayer he wishes.

Some of the terminology that is used in the twelve step programs may have a non-Jewish flavor, but this does not reflect on the content. (Indeed, one person told me that A.A. or O.A. was non-Jewish because they talked about having faith in G-d!) The substance of the twelve steps seems to be not only compatible with Jewishness, but seems to be taken *en toto* out of classical Jewish ethical works. I cannot elaborate on this theme here.

Now to the problem itself. Bulemia is a complex disease, the result of a combination of a number of causative factors. Some cases may have a component of a biochemical factor similar to that producing depression, and in these cases anti-depressant medication may be helpful.

When food is eaten for its nutrient value, eating disorders do not develop. Animals in their natural habitat do not become obese, nor do they binge and regurgitate. Eating disorders come about when people begin using food as a drug rather than as a nutrient.

Hunger is probably the first distress experienced by a human being, and food is the first relief of this distress. The impression that food relieves distress may later extend itself to discomforts other than hunger. In other words, *food can become a tranquilizer*. Why this occurs with some people and not with others is unclear. When circumstances in later life result in emotional distress, some people may seek relief via the first tranquilizer that was known to them: food.

Food is a very ineffective tranquilizer. Firstly, its effects are very short-lived, so that frequent doses are necessary. Secondly, some people feel guilty for relieving their stress with food, and this guilt generates more distress and hence more demand for the tranquilizer, resulting in a vicious cycle. Finally, because it may result in unwanted weight gain, recourse to food may result in misery.

Probably the most common cause of distress resulting in recourse to tranquilizers — whether food or drug — is the feeling of inadequacy or unworthiness: low self-esteem. At the risk of over-generalization, I believe that people turn to food when they feel that *gratification from relationships is in jeopardy.* These relationships fall into two major categories: G-d and people. The person may fear that "G-d does not love me" and "other people do not love me" because "*I am unlovable.*" A bit of self-analysis will reveal that this feeling goes all the way back to childhood, and is invariably the result of erroneous juvenile thoughts and perceptions.

"But," you may say, "I know my husband does love me, and he is the most important person in the world to me. I am not afraid of being unloved."

We know that when a person has a delusional conviction, all the reassurances in the world cannot eradicate it. You may indeed feel assured when your husband asserts how much he loves you, but that reassurance is short-lived, and a nagging doubt, probably even subconscious, soon creeps in. Furthermore, in the average day we do many things that are imperfect, and in the presence of low self-esteem, these can take on gigantic proportions and become additional evidence of inadequacy.

In spite of your husband's reassurances and concrete demonstrations of his love for you, you must realize that you lived with this person for seven years without revealing that you had an eating disorder, and you were obviously afraid, "What would he think of me if he ever found out?"

Just as there are a number of components in the genesis of an eating disorder, there a number of things that must be done to correct it. You will find out more about them in O.A. and in therapy, but I must stress that building self-esteem is of prime importance. In my book *Self-Discovery and Recovery* (Hazelton 1984), I pointed out that following the twelve steps of the anonymous fellowships can help in building self-esteem.

There is a close relationship between feeling loved by other people and feeling loved by G-d. This is clearly stated in the Talmud (*Ethics of the Fathers* 3:13). The more we are able to feel that we are loved by G-d, the more capable we are of feeling loved by others.

G-d's love for us is unconditional. Even at times when He is displeased with us, His love for us is not diminished. He realizes that when we are not obedient to Him, it is due to our folly. As a parent of a five-year-old child, you have certainly had times when your child did something you had forbidden, and although you scolded or even spanked him, your anger did not detract from your love. G-d's love for you is far greater than even the most intense love of a parent for a child, and even when He disciplines us His love for us is boundless.

Most people, except for parents of small children, rarely experience unconditional love. Even with our own children, when they grow older and we can no longer attribute their misbehavior to immaturity, our love tends to become more conditional. Certainly with other people, even with spouses, love tends to be conditional on their pleasing us.

We can accept being loved unconditionally to the extent that we are capable of loving others unconditionally. In our relationship to G-d, this is manifested by *mesiras nefesh*, by our willingness to give ourselves over totally to G-d. We look to our forefather, the patriarch Abraham, as the prototype whom we are to emulate, and while we may be unable to attain the perfection of Abraham, his unconditional love for G-d, which withstood the severest of tests, is the ultimate goal for which we shall strive.

The dictum of King Solomon, "As water reflects one's image, so does the feeling of one heart reflect another" (*Proverbs* 27:19) confirms this. If we are capable of loving others unconditionally, we can accept being loved unconditionally. The latter is important, because as fallible human beings, we all have imperfections.

The problem of low self-esteem, however, is not that we feel inadequate because of the factual imperfections within us. That would be a rather simple problem. The difficulty is that we feel inadequate or unworthy without just cause, and it takes considerable effort to overcome this.

A competent therapist can be of great help. However, a psychologist who has not had experience with eating disorders may not be able to adequately untangle the various problems involved in this condition. Ask people in O.A. for the name of a therapist who has demonstrated competence in the field.

Among the great works of *chassidus* and *mussar* there are many thoughts that can enhance self-esteem. It is important, however, to have guidance in learning these. Some of these writings, which contain disciplinary material, are subject to distortion which can result in the lowering of one's self-esteem. With a proper instructor, you can derive much strength from learning ways in which to draw yourself closer to G-d by fulfillment of *mitzvos* and in prayer. The awareness that one is fulfilling one's mission on earth can provide a feeling of worthiness that is so crucial to self-esteem.

Correspondence 36

. . .I am now 29, and while I did not have an intensive yeshiva education, I did learn for a while, and I am *shomer Shabbos*.

I began college at 21, and was planning on pursuing a degree in business administration. At college, I met a girl with whom I fell in love. She was from a non-observant home, but was interested in Yiddishkeit, and gradually became a *baalas teshuvah*. Her parents objected to this, and they took a dislike to me because I had influenced her in her decision to become observant. However, they really never took a stand, sort of humoring her and assuming she would revert to their lifestyle when I dropped out of the picture. When they discovered we were serious about each other and were about to become engaged, they hit the ceiling. Although Danielle* did love me, she was unable to stand up to her domineering father, and we broke off. This was four years ago.

I have never recovered from this loss. I still love Danielle, even though I know it is all for nothing, because two years ago she married. I have not been able to do anything with myself. I dropped out of school and took a job, but I have not been able to do well at

---

* Name has been changed.

work, and have had four jobs since. My head is just not operating, and I have no interest in anything.

In desperation, I started smoking marijuana, but even that did not do the trick. After several months I stopped, and I have not used any pot for over a year. I don't miss it. I don't want anything except Danielle, whom I know I can never have.

I have thought of seeing a psychiatrist, but what good would that do? Even he could not restore Danielle to me. My parents have been reading your books, and they suggested that I write to you for advice.

 Whereas the loss of a love relationship can be deeply painful, it is really no different than other major losses, and results in a grief reaction. There are several phases in a grief reaction, generally following the pattern described by Kubler-Ross in her book, *On Death and Dying*. There is a common denominator to grief reactions, which is that there is eventually closure with detachment from the lost object, and life goes on with adjustment to reality. When such detachment does not occur and the reaction persists far beyond the average time, one must suspect that there is something other than a grief reaction that is operative. You are certainly aware that many other people have suffered from frustrated romances, yet have managed to go on with life, and we must speculate on why you have not been able to do so.

Sometimes there is no closure to a grief reaction because there is no real detachment. The Talmud tells us that this is why Jacob never emerged from his grief for Joseph (*Genesis* 37:34-35). Detachment, they say, is possible only from one who has died, but not when the person who is assumed to have died is still alive. It is evident from the *Midrash* that although Jacob consciously assumed Joseph to be dead, he had an intuition that Joseph was still living, hence detachment and termination of the grief was impossible. This is not applicable in your case. Danielle is married, and that is absolutely final.

Sometimes what appears to be a grief reaction is in reality something else. As painful as a loss by death is, it is not a rejection. The loss of a broken romance, however, is usually a rejection, unless the separation is by mutual agreement. To a person with a low self-esteem, such a rejection can be extremely distressful because it reinforces and aggravates one's feeling of unworthiness and inadequacy. It is actually this painful feeling of low self-esteem which has been intensified by the rejection that depresses a person, although he continues to believe that it is the loss of the loved one. The loss is in reality the trigger or the spark, which has initiated a process that can continue after the spark has been extinguished.

This may not account for your difficulty, since Danielle did not really reject you. She was simply not able to detach from her parents, and she undoubtedly suffered as much as you did. It is therefore not likely to be a feeling of having been rejected that is causing your continuing difficulty.

There is another dynamic which may constitute the real problem, and one that I have seen with some frequency. A person with low self-esteem who lacks self-confidence and is terribly afraid of failure, may choose to avoid failure by not undertaking anything. "If you don't try, you cannot fail." One way to avoid failing at something is upon awakening in the morning, simply draw the covers over your head and remain in bed until late in the afternoon. Of course, not doing anything constitutes the greatest failure of all, but for some reason, passive failure seems easier to accept than active failure.

While some people actually retreat into a state of doing nothing, most people consider this reprehensible. They recognize this as indolence or cowardliness, and as much as they fear action, they cannot resign themselves to frank inaction.

This is where the human mind does one of its many tricks. The human defensive systems, both the physical and the psychological, are unbelievably keen and clever, and function to prevent the person from experiencing pain. The avoidance of pain is not always to the person's advantage, as is indicated, for example, by the body's reaction to joint pain, where the reflex splinting of the muscles and the scar tissue that is formed in the joint may relieve the severe pain caused by the movement within the joint, but results in the loss of mobility. Psychologically, too, the unconscious defense mechanisms operate to reduce pain, but this may be at great cost.

What may happen in the person who fears to act because of anticipation of failure, is that the mind seeks out or creates a logical reason why one cannot or should not act. The inaction is thereby justified by rationalization, and the person need not detest oneself as being indolent or cowardly. He now has "legitimate" reason for not acting.

What happens, then, is a subtle reversal of cause and effect. The person thinks up a reason ("a") which he assumes to be responsible for his inability to act ("b"): i.e., he sees "a" as being the cause of "b", and "a" is the culprit. If one accepts this reasoning, one then tries to eliminate "a", which is considered to be the cause. This is invariably unsuccessful, because "a" is *not* the true cause, but merely a rationalization to conceal the real cause, which is the anxiety over the anticipation of failure ("c").

It is easy for a therapist to fall into a trap, because the rationalizations may be very convincing. Months, if not years, of therapy can be spent on trying to eliminate "a", when what should really be addressed is "c".

Let me share an interesting experience with you. Many years ago I was involved in treating a patient, and I was frustrated with the lack of progress. Then, in a relaxing reverie, I recalled an incident of my childhood which illuminated the therapeutic problem.

When I was a child, we would spend several weeks in the summer at a bungalow adjacent to a lake. I loved to go rowboating, but I was not permitted to be out on a boat unaccompanied by an adult. My passion for rowing was so great, that I would get into the boat while it was securely tethered to the pier, and row to my heart's content. Of course, I could not go anywhere since the boat was tied. *The fact that I was tied to the pier made rowing safe*. If the rope were to be untied, and I could move out on the lake, I could be in great danger.

When I recalled this scene, I then realized what was happening with my patient. This young man was very anxious about moving out into life because of a very intense fear that he would fail. He therefore tied himself to a pier ("a") which then allowed him to go through the motion of doing things but never getting anywhere ("b"). I had fallen into the trap of believing "a" to be the cause. After I recognized this and totally avoided dealing with "a" in therapy, (much to my patient's disappointment), and instead dealt with his inordinate anxiety regarding possible failure ("c"), we were able to make progress.

I suspect that the loss of Danielle, which you see as the cause of your inability to function, is in fact a rationalization. The grief reaction over her loss should long since have subsided, but you may be using the loss as a logical explanation to yourself and to others why you cannot advance in life.

Low self-esteem is often the culprit in a majority of people's problems, and is invariably due to a distorted self-perception. Correction of the self-perception can go a long way in eliminating the anxiety about failure, and allow you to adapt to the reality of life, which is, in the final analysis, that life is composed of successes and failures. We enjoy our successes, and while we are distressed over failures, the fear of failure need not be paralytic. It is only when one's self-esteem is so fragile that a failure is perceived as a devastating calamity that one resorts to desperate tactics to avoid it.

I therefore suggest that you have an evaluation with a psychologist especially qualified in management of self-esteem problems, and I will be happy to provide you with several names of therapists in your area.

Correspondence 37

I am thirty-two years old, married, and a mother of three children, ages two, six, and ten. We are a *frum* family, very much "yeshivish." My husband goes to a *daf yomi* learning group daily. He has a small business, and while we are far from wealthy, we are by no means destitute. Money is not our problem, although my husband thinks it is.

My husband was well accepted by my family, which is why his attitude mystifies me. About two years into our marriage, after our first child was born, he began objecting to my contact with my family. First he did not want me to see them quite as often, then not more than once a month, I thought this demand was crazy, but I gave in. Gradually he began objecting to my talking with my mother on the phone.

When we married, my name did not go on our checking account. Although most of my friends write checks, it did not seem worthwhile making a fuss about, but it has become an inconvenience. When I ask him why, he says that two people writing checks on the same account results in too many mistakes. I suggested my having a separate account, but he said we don't have enough money for that. I do not have any charge cards, because he says that buying on credit is too expensive.

After a while I started a small business which I run from my home, and he insisted that I turn all the income over to him. To keep peace in the family, I did. But he is never satisfied. He is a person with a violent temper, and although he has never struck me, his tongue lashings are almost as bad. I don't want to provoke him both for my own sake and to avoid the children witnessing such a scene.

To everyone else he appears to be model person. He is respected by his friends. I think he is a very unhappy person, although I have tried my best to make him happy. I feel like I am in a prison, and I have cried myself to sleep more than once.

Once when his mood was better, I told him there was something wrong with our marriage and that we should see someone for counseling. He dismissed that as foolishness, and let me know that if I sought counseling for myself he would not pay for it. I have thought of doing so and asking my parents to pay, but I am afraid of his reaction if they did. My parents may sense that I am unhappy, but we have never discussed it, especially since I speak to them so infrequently.

I have thought of talking to our *rav*, but I am afraid he will think I am crazy. To him, my husband appears to be a *tzaddik,* who is always at *minyan,* at *daf yomi,* gives *tzedakah* and never turns down a request for help. Maybe he is a *tzaddik,* but does the wife of a *tzaddik* have to live in torture?

I'm stuck, and I don't know what to do.

Let us begin with a primary principle. *There is no justification for a woman to suffer emotional abuse any more than physical abuse.* Some women have found ways to justify even tolerating physical beatings, and many more have resigned themselves to emotional abuse, Not only is this a grievous mistake for oneself, but it is also not a healthy example for children, who are very sensitive and can easily detect what is happening. If your sons model themselves after their father and your daughters after you, you are providing for three potentially very unhappy couples.

I am not sitting in judgment on your case, which would require me to listen to both sides, because there is always the possibility of the account given by one spouse being a distortion. I am going to respond on the assumption that your description is valid. In the event that your particular version happens to be distorted, there are nevertheless cases where such conditions do prevail, and the information I am going to provide will be helpful to others, inasmuch as I intend to publish my responses to such inquiries.

Contrary to popular assumption, cases of wife abuse are not rare among Jews. Traditionally, it had been assumed that Jewish husbands are considerate and never abusive. Whether this is myth or whether things have changed drastically after we left the *shtetl* and began to adapt customs and practices of the non-Jewish environment in which we find ourselves, is something which I do not know.

Women who have absorbed abuse give various reasons for their doing so. If they are familiar with Torah, they quote the Talmudic statement that "A virtuous woman is one who does her husband's will." Obviously this has its limitations, and no observant woman would invoke this Talmudic statement, for example, as a rationale to cook for her husband on Shabbos if he so desires. Someone who learns *daf yomi* should know the Talmudic guidelines for relating to one's wife: "Love her as you love yourself, respect her more than you respect yourself." Violation of this is no less a transgression than violation of any other halachah.

While I cannot diagnose any one *in absentia*, I have had direct exposure to people with a personality such as you describe of your husband. It is possible to give such people a psychiatric diagnosis, but I do not wish to focus on him, rather on you. It is not uncommon to impugn the victim, and what I am about to say should not be misinterpreted as blame.

Let me begin with a psychological principle. For all practical purposes, no one can change anyone else, and it is generally futile to try. A person can only make changes in himself.

While you see your husband as the aggressor, which he indeed appears to be, the Talmud *Gittin* 45a states the principle "It is not the mouse that is the thief, but it is rather the hole where it hides that is the thief. If it were not that it had a place to hide, it would not steal." According to this, the passive hole in the wall which has done nothing is a major accomplice in the theft.

In any abusive relationship, there are two participants: one who does the abusing, and one who allows oneself to be abused. It is further characteristic that abuse problems become more complex as they continue. For example, the dilemma you face with the possibility of a non-viable marriage is a much more difficult one, now that there are three children than it was when there was only one child.

Whatever method might be employed, there must be one firm and unyielding position you must take: *"I do not deserve to be abused, and I will not continue to take abuse."* What you will do and how you will do it remains to be elaborated, but all your behavior until now reflects a lack of this conviction. Everything you do from now on must be based on this premise: "My self-respect is not negotiable." There are some risks you will have to take, there may be some unpleasant scenes, and there may be actions you may have to take that you would prefer to avoid, but nothing should stand in the way of your refusing to be abused. Perhaps you may think it is virtuous to be a martyr, but the Torah condemns human sacrifice and as I said, you are also providing an unhealthy example for your children,

Firstly, you should not be standing alone. If you have caring parents, you should take them into your confidence. They will likely have to help you pay for your counseling, which you will undoubtedly need.

Your concern that your husband may become enraged if you tell your parents or seek counseling is certainly understandable, but you cannot allow yourself to be terrorized. If he rants and raves, you simply must be firm and keep your cool. Thus far, according to you he has never harmed you physically, but there is no guarantee that if sufficiently provoked he will not do so. Should he threaten to do so, you should make it clear to him that you will summon the police and press charges of assault. If you are hesitant to do so because you wish to avoid a scandal or stigmatize the family, or because you think it will be a *chilul Hashem,* then you must resign yourself to being at his mercy for the rest of your life. Do not voice the above threat unless you are ready to execute it. If you are truly ready to do so, he will get the message.

Of course, every effort should be made to preserve a viable marriage, if it is indeed viable. There is a possibility that a husband who has been tyrannical may change and that the relationship can be a happy and wholesome one, but there must be adequate reason for him to change. He will not change as long as his way of doing things continues to work for him. It is therefore your job to make him understand in no uncertain terms that the current situation is not going to continue. It would be foolish to expect dramatic changes to occur overnight, but given time and effort, a favorable change can occur.

However, you must be in a position of maximum strength. If your husband were to indicate that he will terminate the marriage if you seek counseling or the help of your parents, then you must be prepared for that. You should consult a suitable lawyer to be aware of your legal rights and what to do to protect yourself economically.

There are competent rabbis who will listen to your problem sympathetically and provide you with guidance on any halachic issues that may arise. A few inquiries as to who are the rabbis that have specialized in abuse problems can lead you to the right person.

After you have taken the preparatory steps, you should tell your parents and begin seeing a counselor or therapist. There is no way to predict your husband's reaction, but you will be ready for whatever transpires and you will have the support of your parents and the guidance of your therapist. Hopefully, your husband's investment in the family will result in his participation, perhaps grudgingly at the beginning, but later more willingly. He may not have the slightest awareness that his current behavior is unacceptable, and it is possible that he may change if he begins to understand this. He may have been suffering from psychological problems which express themselves in this way, and he may see the need to seek help for himself.

There is much reason for hope that your marriage can be a very satisfactory one, but not on the present terms. Obviously your husband is not going to institute any change, so that any change that is going to occur must begin with you. If you do so with support and guidance there may be a very favorable outcome.

Correspondence 38

. . .I am turning to you for advice. Perhaps you can guide me.

My wife and I raised two wonderful children. My son is happily married and lives at some distance from us. My daughter divorced two years ago, and about this time she began seeing a psychiatrist. We had been very close, but she began to distance herself from us. She no longer comes to visit, and phone calls have become very brief and abrupt. As this continued, I asked her what was happening, and she broke loose with a tirade that left me speechless: accusations of how we mistreated her and things she said we did that were frank lies. She said that her psychiatrist had opened her eyes to the "truth".

I promptly called the psychiatrist and I have persisted in my efforts to contact him, but he has never returned my calls. I mentioned this to a psychologist friend of mine, and he said that a psychiatrist has a confidential relationship with his patient and that some psychiatrists feel that it is a violation of this confidentiality to talk with a family member without the patient's permission.

What I cannot understand is how a psychiatrist can condemn a person without giving him a chance to defend himself. How would the psychiatrist feel if a patient accused him of indecent behavior, and someone took action against him without giving him the opportunity to deny the accusation or defend himself? You might say that my daughter's accusations against me are not of a criminal nature, but that is really irrelevant. She has turned against us or has been turned against us, and is depriving herself as well as us of an important relationship. Her psychiatrist is actively aiding and abetting this, and I cannot see how this is ethically permissible.

Did we make mistakes in raising our children? I am sure we did. After all, we don't have the opportunity to raise children when we are older and wiser. Our childbearing years are when we are young and inexperienced.

I am asking you for advice on what I can do to save our family. I have been very impressed with your approach in *Living Each Day* and *Growing Each Day*, and since I am sure that you do not practice this kind of psychiatry, perhaps you can tell me what to do.

 I am deeply moved by your distress. I think back to the years of my residency in psychiatry when I was taught that my relationship must be solely with the patient, and that I would be sabotaging the therapeutic relationship if I had any contact with the family. I was also taught that whether an incident that the patient reports actually happened in real life or not is immaterial. If the patient believed it happened, the emotional effects of a fantasied incident are identical to those of a factual incident, and this had to be dealt with in therapy as a fact. The name given to this phenomenon was "psychic reality," and in my impressionable days as a young resident, the fact that it had a name and that it was taught by my eminent professors led me to accept the validity of this concept. It was not too long before better judgment set in, and now that I can understand what was really meant by "psychic reality," I no longer impale people on the testimony of patients.

Patient confidentiality is indeed inviolable, but when it is necessary to have contact with the family, I simply tell the patient, "Look. I cannot proceed with therapy without being in touch with your family. I will not reveal anything you tell me in confidence, but if you have any accusations against them, we should meet together so that I can get a grasp on what really happened, and whether this is possibly a distortion in your perception of things."

Unfortunately, your daughter's psychiatrist has taken an approach of which I disapprove. Even in the days when I was a resident, when the purist theory of not jeopardizing the doctor-patient relationship prevailed, there was a social worker on staff who met with the family and served as an intermediary between the doctor and the family. If your daughter's psychiatrist chose not to return your calls, at the very least he could have suggested to you to see someone with whom he could then be in contact.

Since the psychiatrist did not suggest this, you should. I recommend that you write a letter to the psychiatrist, stating that you understand that he may not wish to jeopardize the therapeutic relationship with your daughter, but that you do have important information which can have a bearing on her treatment. Tell him you would like him to recommend a person to whom you can relate, and who would then be in contact with him. This is really your only option. If he refuses to do this, you must sit back and hope that one day your daughter will come to her senses.

The distress you are experiencing is more than enough, without your adding to it with feelings of guilt. All parents can look back and see how they would have done things differently, given the experience that they now have. Raising children was never a simple task, but in the days when the community was smaller, the family unit more cohesive, authority more respected, and discipline more accepted, the challenge was far less than in today's chaotic world. I have repeatedly pleaded that during the junior and senior years of high school, boys and girls be given information on proper parenting. There are excellent resources available for such courses, which could help avoid common mistakes in child-rearing. I assume that you and your wife did your utmost in trying to raise your children in the best possible manner, and even when we have regrets, we should not have feelings of guilt.

I believe we have allowed the philosophy of the commercial world to impact too greatly on our personal lives. In commerce, "good" and "bad" are decided by success and failure respectively. No one is really concerned how or why a person went into a particular business venture. If the bottom line is profitable, it was a good one. If the bottom line is in red, the venture was bad.

We should remember that in our personal, ethical, and moral lives, commercial philosophy is not valid. None of us can predict outcome, and we can only do the best we can with the information we have at hand. When we have done this, we have done what is "good", and even if things do not turn out the way we would have wished, we may be unhappy about a particular result, but there should not be any feelings of guilt.

If your daughter's psychiatrist does not recommend someone to see as an intermediary, it may nevertheless be advisable for you to see someone on your own to help you cope with this very stressful and distressful situation.

Correspondence 39

We have been married fourteen years. My husband spent two years in *kollel* after we were married and is a fine *ben Torah*. He then went into his father's business, and we are financially comfortable. We have four lovely children, ages 12, 10, 6, and 2.

I am trying to trace things back, but I may not be accurate. Approximately five or six years ago, my husband's drinking underwent a change. Instead of just the *kiddush* wine and a little *schnapps* after the fish, his drinking increased. Two beers at each Shabbos meal became the routine. I said nothing because it caused no problem.

Eventually things changed. The two beers became three and four, sometimes even five. Occasionally he falls asleep before *bentching* (blessing after meals), and sometimes he becomes cantankerous. I told him I disapprove of his drinking, but he turns a deaf ear to me.

Recently he has begun to drink beer almost every night, because he says it helps him sleep. It is only one or two beers at night, and this does not affect him adversely. He goes to business everyday, and he is the nicest person you want to know, but Shabbos has become a disaster. He sometimes says very mean things to me on Friday night. When I tell him about his behavior the next day he says I am making all this up. He has no memory of what he said. Incidentally, he never drives after drinking.

I don't like the children seeing their father fall asleep at the table. The children have stopped asking friends over for Shabbos meals because of their father's unpredictable behavior, which embarrasses them.

I don't think my husband is an alcoholic, but I do know that his drinking is a problem, and he refuses to acknowledge this. What can I do?

You say that your husband has a drinking problem but is not an alcoholic. What is an alcoholic?

An alcoholic is a person who in spite of the fact that alcohol causes undesirable effects on himself or others, nevertheless continues to drink. The idea that an alcoholic is the stereotype town *shikkur* (drunkard) lying in the gutter is completely false. It is also not true that Jews are not alcoholics. In my experience, I have encountered Jewish doctors, lawyers, housewives, and yes, even rabbis who are alcoholics. There are various types of alcohol problems and drinking patterns, and various degrees in each. The pattern you describe in your husband is not an uncommon one.

The person with a drinking problem is usually unable to recognize this. It may seem absurd, but even gross disasters secondary to drinking may not break through this denial.

The effects on you and your children should not be minimized. A drinking parent may be very loving, but the children are harmed nevertheless. The children being embarrassed about their father's behavior and their inability to invite friends to the home can have a negative impact on them.

230 □ I AM I

There are several things you must do. Firstly, stop being afraid of the word "alcoholic." Alcoholism is a disease whose cause or causes remain essentially unknown. Your husband is not a bad person but a sick person. Furthermore, you did not cause him to have an alcohol problem, although he may tell you otherwise.

Secondly, you must become knowledgeable about this disease. I suggest you immediately read the book, *Co-Dependent No More*, by Melody Beatty, and my book, *Caution: Kindness Can Be Dangerous to the Alcoholic*. It is now out of print, but can be found in the library.

Thirdly, join an Alanon family group. They are listed in the telephone directory. This group is comprised of family members, predominantly spouses, that share their experiences in living with a person who has an active drinking problem, as well as the experiences in recovery. There is no reason for you to learn things the hard way, when you can benefit from the experience of others.

Fourthly, contact a family therapist who is qualified in alcoholism problems. You may get a referral by calling any of the established treatment centers located in the "Yellow Pages." In addition to getting valuable counseling for yourself and the children, it may be feasible to arrange an "intervention," or a confrontation, to break through your husband's denial. This would have to involve your husband's family, who should be appropriately apprised of the problem.

You may have a concern that taking these steps may expose your husband's alcohol problem and cause embarrassment to the family. You should be aware that exposure of alcoholism is unavoidable, because as the alcohol problem progresses, which it invariably does, your husband will eventually do something which will cause a much greater disgrace than seeking the appropriate help.

Do not delude yourself that things will get better by themselves, because untreated alcoholism gets worse instead of better. Alcoholism is a treatable condition, and with proper treatment, recovery can bring relief to everyone and result in a happy family life.

Correspondence 40

. . .Like many of my friends, I was searching for something, and on a trip to Israel I was introduced to a *baal teshuvah* yeshivah, where I have studied for the past two years. Someone here gave me your book, *Let Us Make Man*, and this is why I am writing to you.

I have been in turmoil since my early adolescence. My father has achieved almost everything to which a person could aspire: wealth, comfort, summer home, you name it. He is highly respected in the community.

However, our home is far from a happy one. My father is constantly dissatisfied, and I suspect my parents' marriage is on the rocks. My older brother is lost somewhere in the San Francisco drug culture, and my older sister is twice divorced at age twenty-seven. It was simple to see that something was missing in our home, and I searched for that missing ingredient.

While I am quite satisfied at my yeshivah, I am still in turmoil. I am looking for the key to peace and tranquility, and while I have not given up the hope of finding it in Torah, I have begun to fear that it may not be there either. I still think I am on the right track, but I am haunted by doubts.

I don't know what led you to think that the key to "peace and tranquility" as they are popularly conceptualized can be found in Torah. I hope I did not convey that idea in my book *Let Us Make Man*. In Torah we find the key to growth, but growth and "tranquility" as the latter is usually understood are not only not identical, but may actually be mutually exclusive.

A number of years ago, books with titles such as, *Peace of Mind* or *Peace of Soul* became popular. Many people were led to believe that "tranquility" is something like *nirvana* which is within human reach. I have no doubt that this misconception was responsible for some people seeking this kind of tranquility in drugs, whether illicit or prescribed.

Rashi states that the patriarch Jacob desired to spend the rest of his life in tranquility, and that G-d said, "Tranquility will be in Paradise, not on Earth," and Jacob was then subjected to the severe torment of the episode of Joseph and his brothers (*Genesis* 37:2). What was so terrible about wishing to live in tranquility that Jacob had to be subjected to the distress of the loss of Joseph?

The ethical works distinguish between angels and humans, and stress that the former are static and the latter are dynamic. Man must grow, and growth does not occur without friction. It is a law of physics that every moving object encounters friction in overcoming resistance to inertia, and energy must be expended in overcoming this resistance. Complete tranquility can occur only when one remains stationary. Jacob was reprimanded by G-d for seeking tranquility because he still had the potential for further spiritual progress, and the latter is incompatible with tranquility. The Scripture states that man was created to toil (*Job* 5:7). If this is indeed the purpose of man's creation, then when man reaches a point where he no longer toils, there is no further purpose for his existence.

There is a dairy company that advertises that its milk comes from "contented cows". The idea behind this claim is that the finest milk comes from cows of superior quality, and the zenith of perfection of a cow is obviously its being content. Those who seek contentment as their goal in life share a goal with cows. I, for one, would be highly insulted to share a goal in life with a cow.

Human beings are created with a *yetzer tov* (good inclination) and a *yetzer hara* (evil inclination). These are constantly at odds, and there is therefore an ongoing struggle throughout a person's lifetime between the two. How can a person possibly envision oneself being "tranquil" or having "peace of mind" when such a situation exists?

Spiritual growth does not come easily. In an era when science and technology have made so many things easy for us, many of us have come to believe that struggle is a thing of the past. Perhaps our physical existence has indeed become more comfortable, but spirituality has not become easier to attain. On the contrary, we must now exert far greater efforts to achieve spiritual growth than in the past.

There were people to whom spirituality was the prime focus of their lives, and nothing else even came close. We are far from that level.

A chassid of Rabbi Uri of Strelisk was unable to raise the money for a dowry for his daughter, and his wife instructed him to ask the Rebbe for a *brachah* (blessing) to succeed in his business so that they could afford a dowry. Every time the chassid came to the Rebbe he became so engrossed in his spiritual growth that he totally forgot to ask for a *brachah*. Finally his wife made him take a solemn oath that he would ask for a *brachah*.

On his next visit to the Rebbe he had no choice but to fulfill his vow, and the Rebbe told him, "When you pray the *Boruch She'amar*, and you come to the verse 'Blessed is He who is merciful to His creations,' remember to ask for a Divine blessing, and your prayers will be answered." The chassid was shocked and exclaimed, "What! In the midst of my prayers I am to think about money?"

There were once people whose aspirations were solely to come closer to G-d, and whereas physical survival was a necessity, they saw it only as a means to a higher goal. Today we seem to have lost sight of this.

A pediatrician keeps candy in his office with which he appeases his juvenile patients so that they will submit to examination and treatment, and when a child comes to the office, he asks the doctor for candy. A mature adult who values life and health will not ask the doctor for a prize. To the contrary, he will pay the doctor handsomely to help him be well. People who know the value of spirituality will feel that asking G-d for material things is like an adult asking the doctor for candy instead of life-saving treatment, and this is unthinkable.

Contentment is having all one's needs met, and the closest we come to it is the infant who has just been fed and drifts off to sleep with a beatific smile on his face. The need to always achieve greater spirituality and to draw oneself nearer to G-d does not allow for such contentment, and a truly spiritual person should not expect it. However, while contentment is not feasible for one who seeks spiritual growth, *happiness* is indeed attainable, if one defines happiness as the feeling that one is actively fulfilling one's purpose in creation.

Your search for meaning in life has fortunately brought you to Torah, but you must be careful not to have unrealistic expectations of Torah. Torah can provide you with happiness, but not with the kind of "tranquility" which modern man seems to be pursuing.

NOTES

NOTES

NOTES

NOTES